# Tennis: Game of Motion

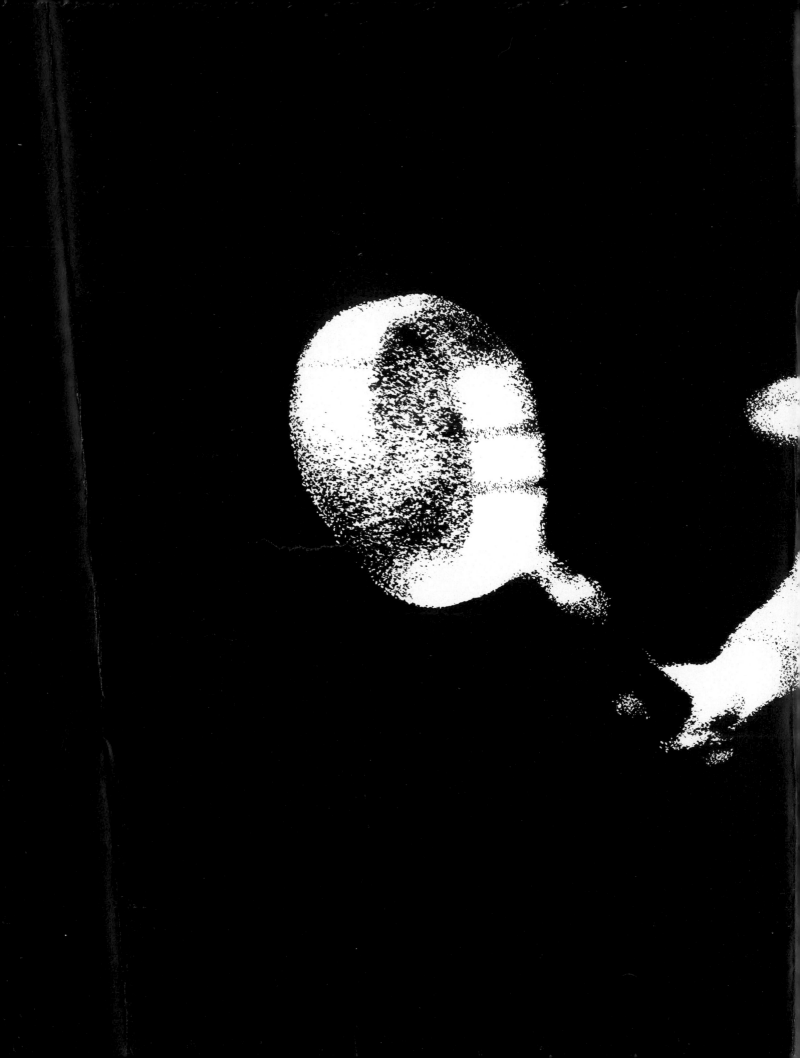

# Tennis: Game of Motion

## by Eugene Scott

A Rutledge Book
Crown Publishers, Inc.
New York, New York 10016

Fred R. Sammis — Publisher
John T. Sammis — Creative Director
Doris Townsend — Editor-in-Chief
Allan Mogel — Art Director
Jeanne McClow — Managing Editor
Jeremy Friedlander — Associate Editor
Gwen Evrard — Associate Art Director
Arthur Gubernick — Production Consultant
Penny Post — Production Manager
Margaret Riemer — Editorial Assistant
Sally Andrews — Editorial Assistant

Library of Congress Catalog Card Number: 72-82972
ISBN : 0—517—658
Prepared and produced by Rutledge Books, Inc., 17 East 45th St., New York, N.Y. 10017.
Published by Crown Publishers, Inc., 419 Park Avenue South, New York, N.Y. 10016.
Published simultaneously in Canada by General Publishing Company, Ltd.

Contents

# 1/ Tennis: A Cult

The motion was a sweeping backhand—a pencil stroke through the name of Ambassador George Bush—spelling default in a friendly doubles tournament. Seemingly an insignificant gesture, it symbolized nevertheless the fanatical tennis fever gripping the country. Having been called to an emergency session of the United Nations Security Council on the day for which his match was scheduled, Bush had telephoned the River Club to explain the conflict. The response was curt: "You can't make it? Sorry, you'll have to default."

Perhaps more revealing than the curt treatment the American ambassador received from local tournament officials was the failure of George Bush to protest even perfunctorily. He was undoubtedly resigned to defeat before he picked up the phone. After all, a game is a game, and that a matter of state was not considered reason enough for postponing a club doubles match is a fair indication of how seriously tennis players take their sport.

Tennis is the renaissance sport of the seventies. For 20 years tennis had paled dismally on the sidelines while its sleeker brother, golf, was creating headlines and establishing folk heroes. Golf, however, accelerated to its glory so rapidly that its popularity has already peaked, whereas tennis, once the unwanted stepchild of recreation, has become the dynamic action of the moment.

Today's people want exercise, and they want it readily accessible. Is it really worth it, they ask, to get up at six on a Saturday morning just to reserve for your foursome a ten o'clock starting time, spend another two hours on drinks and lunch and return home having had less exercise than a brisk hour's walk would have supplied? Recent efforts to make tennis-court surfaces more attractive indicate that the aesthetic instincts which galvanized golfers are finally being catered to in tennis. New indoor facilities, synthetic courts and revolutionary racquet equipment assure tennis its lofty parapet as the participant sport of this decade.

Naturally, the new fanaticism over tennis has produced some weird behavior. A millionaire oil executive recently pursued a national doubles ranking in the obscure junior veterans category with overpowering single-mindedness. To satisfy United States Lawn Tennis Association (USLTA) ranking requirements, his odyssey carried him 5,000 miles to tournaments in New Hampshire and Florida.

*Tennis has shed its mantle of exclusivity and become a broad-based sport of the masses. Its city playground facilities are a far cry from the pomp and elegance of the early French courtyards.*

A month later, another prominent capitalist paid an aging tennis pro $1,000 to be his partner in the veterans doubles at Wimbledon. He discovered, to his dismay, that four other businessmen had hired prominent pros for the same event. These incidents of tennis mania are not isolated. A respected New York art dealer will play tennis on a clay court only. He insists that hard surfaces have caused arthritis in his knees. Furthermore, he will play only with pressureless Swedish Tretorn balls, which reduce the speed of groundstrokes and favor the finicky artman with his loblike serve.

Even expert players are not exempt from idiosyncrasies. Former Wimbledon champion Dick Savitt invites prominent pros to Jamaica during his vacation because he fears he won't get adequate practice otherwise. His desperation is not unique. Many club players arrive with their own sparring mates or organize a tournament at their vacation spot for the same reason. It doesn't happen in any other sport.

Current tennis fever is characterized by two phenomena. One is its epidemiclike growth. According to a Nielsen survey, 11 million people now play tennis, and the figure will grow to 16 million by 1980. The other is the intensely serious attitude of the current 11 million. No player takes his tennis lightly.

The passion for tennis today has a broad base. Because of the game's standard all-white uniform, the construction worker and the advertising executive playing beside one another in Central Park are indistinguishable except perhaps for hairstyle and arm size. Gone are the days when long flannel pants and a racquet with a green stain (indicating play on grass courts) in the center of the strings were *de rigueur*. Early tennis was played on grass, which was almost symbolic of the cleanliness and tidiness of those who played. The sport did not wear off on its participant. The finely manicured grass courts of Eastern establishment clubs provide luxury for a mere handful of tennis players now.

The rest of the 11 million play on either cement or a granular derivative of common clay. The latter is simply called "dirt" in Europe. "Pietrangeli was wild on dirt but nothing on the fast stuff" meant that the great Italian, who won two French titles on clay, was an ordinary player on grass or cement. Dirt, perhaps, best characterizes the irrational frenzy that is tennis, for it is im-

*Tennis generates in a player a full range of emotions and moods—a feeling of capriciousness by the game itself, of solitude created by its being an individual's sport and of despondency that always comes with losing in any competition.*

The "lawn" in lawn tennis has become
all but extinct, having been replaced by
all-weather, maintenance-free surfaces.

Spectators now flock to watch
professional tennis matches. There
galleries can identify and mingle
with their heroes in an
informal atmosphere not associated
with baseball or football,
where bastion-type stadiums separate
athletes from fans with crude screens
and endless walls of cement.

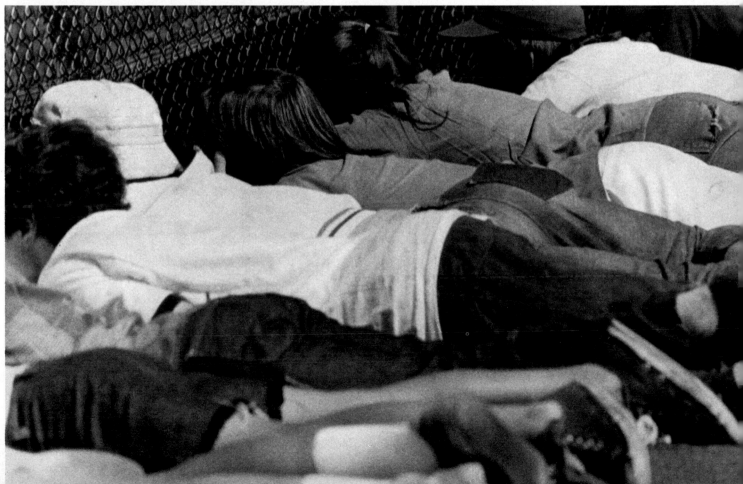

nor excessive. Tennis players, in fact, were once reputed to be such cheapskates that the balls they would buy in April were said to be still around at the end of the season. There are countless stories justifying players' parsimonious reputations. One tells of a Piping Rock Club heiress who collected used tennis balls, which she sent to the American Novelty Corporation in company-provided laundry bags. Each held 100 balls, and the heiress got a nickel for each ball. In another account of thriftiness, the editor of a popular tennis publication was so infuriated by the stinginess of a certain advertiser that she cropped the company-identifying trademark from the action shots of players in her magazine.

Another similarity between the country club and public court player is that both take more time in selecting tennis equipment than in choosing a lawyer or doctor. It's not unusual for a duffer to spend an hour in a tennis shop examining 50 frames, testing the balance, weight and grip size of each as well as its string tension and cosmetic appeal before choosing a model that except for paint and decal application is identical to the first racquet he inspected.

Society's present emphasis on speed and economy has accelerated interest in tennis, which affords quick exercise cheaply. As a result, a new breed of "second generation athletes" has developed. These men, who begin playing tennis at 40, have to learn quickly and without the luxury of lessons; their form is often primitive. Elegance is sacrificed when one player confronts another, adding ferocity to the fanaticism. Playing badly in golf is not a demeaning experience. Losing to your business partner in tennis is.

It's not easy to explain why tennis brings out fanatical behavior more than other sports do. Partly, it is because the game is difficult to learn. Try playing with the opposite hand, and you'll get an idea of how bewildering tennis is for beginners. It takes years of practice just to reach mediocrity. It is difficult for a beginner to sustain a rally, and socking balls into the net or out of the court is frustrating. A beginner must decide whether he wants to emphasize form, power or steadiness; this dilemma is described by a facetious nineteenth-century definition of the serve as "hitting one ball hard into the net and dropping another gently over it."

ponderable why a modern athlete spoiled by synthetic grass, lush carpets and tartan turf would enjoy playing on dirt. Five years ago, public cement courts were rarely used outside California. Now the municipal courts in almost every major city are booked for the day, and there is a growing demand for more courts.

The country club and the public court player have similar habits. Both are notoriously thrifty. Neither has ever been exposed to the extravagance of golf, where $15 for a greens fee and three balls a round per player are considered neither unusual

Above: *Old lions, Gonzalez and Ulrich, commune at Forest Hills.*
Opposite: *Rarely do athletes accept fortune or lack of fortune in silence.*

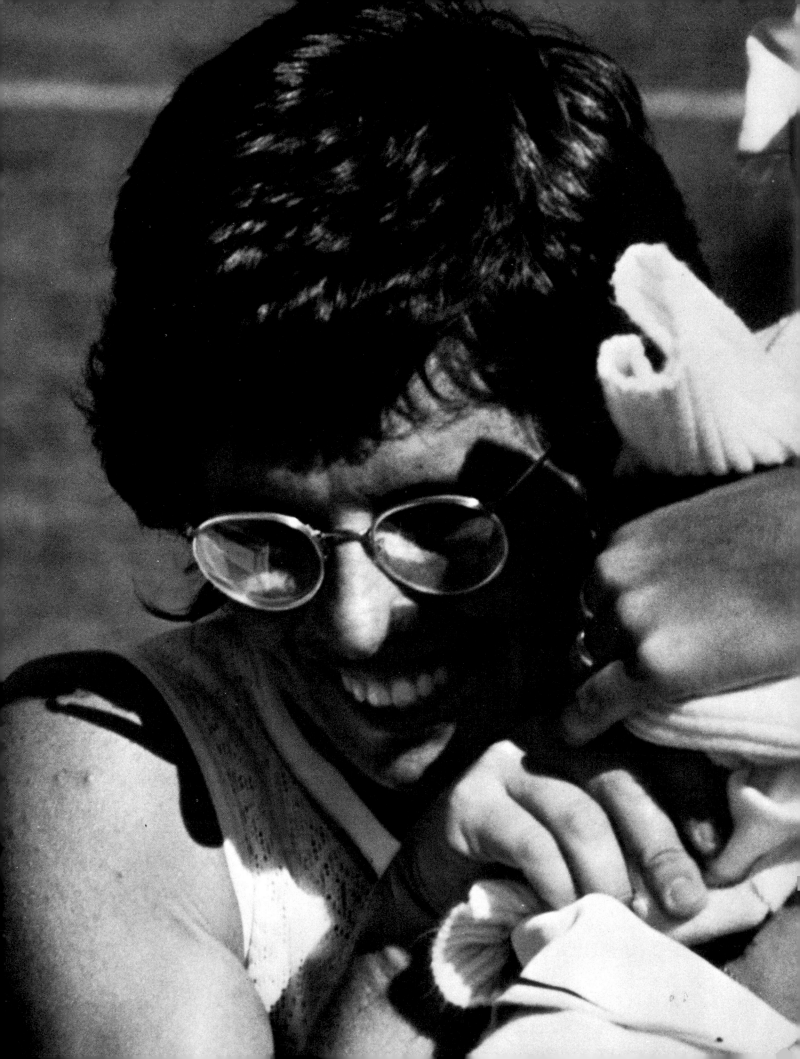

More clinically, the frustration unique to tennis is, perhaps, the product of face-to-face competition without the tension-freeing moments that are part of golf's relaxed pace. A magnificent three-iron hit next to the pin is protected and secure; your opponent can't take the shot away from you. However, in tennis you can bury a forehand into a corner and have the shot rendered harmless by a good retrieve and a high lob. The interplay between a bold topspin stroke and the emasculating defensive slice can sour the most pleasant disposition.

The isolation of an athlete playing singles is complete. He is all alone; he cannot call for assistance from a teammate. By himself, he must decide whether to attack his opponent's forehand or to retreat and lob to the baseline. His performance is measured by his ability to respond to a counterpunch. Success or failure is determined by prowess alone, without physical contact. In football or hockey the frustration of failure can be spent in a crushing tackle or vicious check. In tennis the only contact is defined by the parabola of rally from one side of the net to the other.

A tennis court has always been a stage. Courts are marked out so that a gallery can watch. For the same reason that the first tee in golf turns big hitters into slicers—or worse, dribblers—all tennis courts are metaphorically first tees. Players must come to terms with spectators observing their awkward strokes; yet seldom do players shrink from

this challenge. At every club there is a number-one court, the show court, where tournament matches and exhibitions are played. Every player, no matter how inexpert, is inexorably drawn to that court even when other courts are available. There are no shrinking violets who prefer to play on the back tier, where their lack of expertise will go unnoticed. On the contrary, the club pro is continually entreated to boot four youngsters off the number-one court onto an unused lower court so that an elderly doubles match may proceed.

Former Davis Cup captain Billy Talbert observes that "there is a unique pressure on any tennis player—both weekender and tournament performer—to accept total responsibility for his performance. There is a direct confrontation across the net with one person in full view of your wife, friends and the public. You have no excuses. Alibis are irrelevant."

The tennis frenzy is unlikely to subside. Tennis is no longer a sport limited to warm climates. There are currently 500 indoor facilities in the United States, a figure that will double every three years for the next ten. And since tennis can be played indoors or outdoors, close to home or close to work, the tennis cult is not restricted to summer or weekends. Golf is not played in winter climates, and generally, during the summer it is played on weekends only. But a men's tennis foursome can be a year-round, daily proposition. And familiarity can fan the fanaticism. The lunch-hour or five-

Preceding pages and opposite: *Billie Jean King emotes freely after her victory.*
Above: *The venerable Newport Casino center court, home of the first National Championships in 1889, now welcomes the Virginia Slims tournament.*

o'clock doubles is as familiar to some New Yorkers as a coffee break. However, brotherhood on the court does not mean brotherhood off the court, and vice versa. Doubles partners may never see the inside of each other's house. Conversely, best friends may have equally good groundstrokes but never play together.

Indoor tennis breeds its own special hysteria. Most profitable indoor tennis centers sell time on an hourly basis. Let's assume that four doctors reserve a four-to-five slot for every Tuesday afternoon during the winter; this routine will demand more discipline than their office schedule, where tardiness means only a delayed appointment. Indoor tennis does not permit the tardy player to recapture lost minutes. And that lost time is expensive. The Vanderbilt Athletic Club in New York City charges $38 an hour, and if you aren't poised in the locker room to spring on court at the end of the hour, you'll be shed as a partner quicker than a wet polo shirt.

Tennis players must learn to live with peculiar strokes. A golfer playing poorly is not ridiculed. His real opponent is par. Two golfers competing have little effect on each other's game. Not so in tennis. Losing to a friend in tennis is demoralizing. Worse, it presents a situation in which guile can

humble technical excellence. One can mechanize a respectable golf swing, but a deftly placed tennis ball can turn a graceful motion into an awkward lunge.

There are psychological elements in the sport that befit the almost maniacal disposition of many participants. For example, in what other sport is cheating an accepted part? Yes, cheating. One can euphemize a footfault as carelessness, but in actual fact a player who is footfaulting has an enormous advantage over one who is not. Sixty percent of club doubles players footfault regularly, and at this level there are no linesmen to observe the infraction. Although most illegal foot movement is unconscious, the opponent is nonetheless being cheated. We are speaking not of a toe barely touching the line but of a giant step in front of the baseline before the server has made contact with the ball. Imagine Rod Laver serving a yard closer to the net!

Golfers like to tell about the duffer who disappears into a bunker and sprays the countryside with jets of sand. Reappearing five minutes later, the duffer blandly reports that in his absence only one stroke was added to his score. Even a thief would be embarrassed to try this more than once a round, but in tennis, calling *in* balls *out* is an

*A sign of tennis's arrival is the appearance of celebrities such as Ethel Kennedy at Forest Hills* (opposite) *and Kirk Douglas, shown participating in friendly doubles on a New York City rooftop* (above).

accepted practice in many circles and may occur several times in a game. In some club games an emergency tactic is to hit down the middle for the sole reason that there is no way to call a ball out when it hits in the middle of the court. In fairness, however, it must be added that 99 percent of tennis players don't consciously fudge on line decisions. But a substantial number can *watch* a ball strike the line and *see* it out. It is as if the player's eyes pick up the ball and place it beyond the line.

The matter is complex, for in no other sport is a player called on to rule against himself so often. In a law court this practice would be prohibited by provisions against self-incrimination. But on a tennis court many balls will land close to the line, and if you are playing properly, you will watch the ball and not the line. If you give the benefit of doubt to your opponent and he eventually wins the point, you are subconsciously annoyed that you gave him a break. If you call a close one against him, your conscience may bother you.

Spectators are not immune to the frenzy of a game that for years had to live down its reputation as a "sissy" sport. South African Davis Cupper Bob Hewitt, after a violent temper display, was attacked by a disapproving 70-year-old artist who delivered a karate blow to the back of Hewitt's neck, knocking him unconscious and out of competition for three months. A New Jersey fan drives 100 miles each day of the U.S. Open at Forest Hills to sit in the stadium seat he has had for 20 years. Two years ago the fan paid an usher $50 to cut down a gigantic tree obstructing his view onto the field courts. It was a monumental landscaping alteration, performed surreptitiously at midnight. No one noticed the change.

Although golf enjoyed enormous popularity in the sixties, there seems to be no great prospect for that sport's expansion when one considers the 200 acres required to construct a course. The potential for expansion in tennis is infinite. And with each new indoor or outdoor court, the lunch-hour doubles will become more and more familiar a ritual. Enthusiasm for tennis was aptly articulated by Supreme Court Justice Hugo Black, who did not view his weakness for a friendly doubles as weakness: "When I was forty, my doctor advised me that a man in his forties shouldn't play tennis. I heeded his advice carefully and could hardly wait until I reached fifty to start again."

Above: *The contrast between perfect symmetry in the ready position and the imbalance of a glorious tumble is striking.* Opposite: *The euphoric daze of Rosewall, captured at the instant of his winning match point against Laver for $50,000 in the WCT finals in Dallas.*

# Reflections

2/

Some sports historians with vivid imaginations and a fondness for trivia like to believe that the first tennis match was between two primates batting a rock back and forth with their hands over a small hill. If so, their palms must have smarted after five sets. Chances are that they eventually wrapped their hands in tiger hide to ease the soreness. Bare hands soon gave way to solid, wood paddles, modified in turn with a catgut mesh. Scoring and rules changed over the centuries, and the court itself went through assorted mutations, but the game remains remarkably similar to its original version.

Precise accounts of the actual beginnings of tennis are spotty but colorful. Some have traced tennis to a Persian civilization of the fifth century B.C. The game *tchigan* was played with long paddles in a space enclosed like a hockey rink. Others, leaning to classical origins, trace tennis to ancient Greece. In Homer's *Odyssey,* for instance, we are told how a certain princess batted a ball back and forth with her handmaidens, the only available opposition. Because the men were waging war, only the ladies had time to play. Tennis is also mentioned in Horace's "Fifth Satire," which revealed that Maecenas "goes to play at tennis while Horace and Vergil sleep."

The Persian account is easier to accept, for it explains the game's journey to France as a chance accompaniment of the Saracen invasion. It also expedites the search for the derivation of the word *tennis* to the French *tenez,* meaning "to play." And it is a fact that tennis, as recognized today, surfaced in France in the thirteenth century. It was known as *jeu de paume* ("game of the palm") and was played with a ball made of layers of cloth bound or sewn into a hard, round shape. *Jeu de paume* was first enjoyed in monastery courtyards, and it grew so popular that in 1245, the archbishop of Rouen prohibited priests from playing because they were ignoring their contemplative duties. Royalty quickly adopted the game. Louis X was the game's first recorded casualty. He played a marathon match at Vincennes, caught pneumonia and died shortly afterward.

During the fourteenth century, tennis was officially banned in both England and France. It had come to England around 1352, when Edward III had a court built inside his palace. Enthusiasm for the sport, however, was not restricted to royalty

and became so widespread that Edward IV had to ban tennis in 1388 because his subjects were forsaking archery for it. At about the same time, during the reign of Charles V in France (1364–80), it was reported that there were more tennis players in Paris than drunkards in England. French citizenry ignored job and family to such an extent that Charles, too, banned the game. Nevertheless, tennis fever continued to rise, and in time tennis was besieged by the plague of all popular sports—gambling. Heavy wagering on matches became so disruptive that public tennis exhibitions were finally banned in France in the early 1600s.

The sport returned to the rich (where for the most part it remained until the second half of the twentieth century). The eighteenth-century name of the game, court tennis or royal tennis, clearly indicates who got to play. Tennis became confined to an elaborate indoor arena consisting of *grilles, dedans* and *tambours*. When the scoring became difficult, an abacus was used. Royal (or court) tennis is still played in the United States, with rules, racquets and crazy-shaped courts identical to those at Henry VIII's favorite hangout, Hampton Court. Two brothers, James C. Bostwick and George H. ("Pete") Bostwick, recently twice battled each other for the world court-tennis title, suggesting the almost incestuous state of the game during the past 300 years.

Tennis was ready for its modern inventor, Major Walter Clopton Wingfield. In 1873, he decided to liven up a monotonous garden party in Wales by introducing lawn tennis to his guests. Actually, the major was an innovator, not an inventor. He combined elements from existing games —court tennis, racquets (a slum game turned snob game at Eton and Harrow) and badminton.

The boundaries of Wingfield's game came from court tennis. His original net was over five feet high at the posts and sloped to less than four feet at the center. The slope of the net was not by design but rather because a straight net was impossible without substantial but unavailable support from the posts. Today's posts must be supported by the equivalent of 200 pounds dead weight to allow the center cable to be pulled tight enough for a net 36 inches high at the center. To ensure rigidity today, most all posts are implanted deep in the ground and sometimes encased in cement (a process hardly feasible in the 1870s).

Wingfield's frolic resulted in the addition of the word *lawn* to the name of the game, the marking out of the court in an hourglass shape, the substitution of a plain rubber ball for the solid-fabric sphere and—most important—the popularization, or repopularization, of the sport. It must be added that although he did popularize tennis, he was pretty pompous about it. At the unveiling of his new game at the Nantclwyd lawn party, he called it "sphairistike" (from a Greek word meaning "to play").

It is not surprising that with its roots buried in snobbish aristocracy, tennis had to struggle mightily to reach the masses. Miss Mary Ewing Outerbridge, of Staten Island, is generally credited with introducing the game to America. Miss Outerbridge vacationed in Bermuda during the early months of 1874 and was so fascinated by Wingfield's concoction that she brought racquets, balls and a net back with her for experimentation at the Staten Island Cricket and Baseball Club. New Englanders, always eager for an argument over tradition, later boasted that tennis was first played in this country at William Appleton's estate in Nahant, Massachusetts. This claim is unsupported.

*The interior of a royal tennis court as it appeared in a book published circa 1589. When points were scored, a "marker" would chalk the scores either on the stone floor or on the wall. The marker also kept track of "chases," which were points given on the basis of the distance from the back wall to the place of the ball's second bounce.*

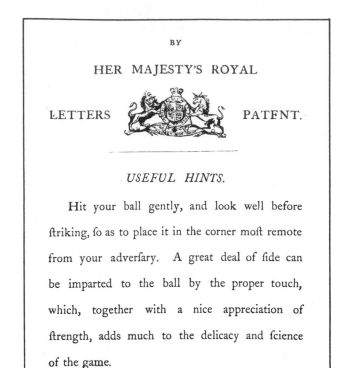

From its humble beginnings as a popular sport at the turn of the twentieth century, tennis droned dully along for years, occasionally enlivened by the fiery personalities of such great stars as Tilden, Borotra, LaCoste, Vines and Budge. It was not until 1968 that all hell would break loose in the sleepy world of the sport. In that year, a game that had previously been directionless would suddenly point in too many directions. But first, let's examine the changes that had taken place in tennis since the beginning.

Until Major Wingfield redefined tennis in 1873, the ball had had basically the same form for a thousand years. Originally the ball consisted of crude cloth strips tightly bound together. Eventually the cloth strips became the core, wrapped in twine and covered by a finer cloth or felt hand-stitched around it. One improvement seems to have been the substitution of the all-cloth core for the human-hair stuffing used in Shakespeare's day. Wingfield adopted the plain rubber ball, the primary advantage of which was that its size, unlike that of its flannel predecessor, was relatively standard. Today's balls are radically different from Wingfield's. Crude Indian rubber forms the core, which is fabricated into two half-grapefruit-shaped sections. The sections are joined to mold the ball, and 18 pounds of pressure are injected to ensure a regular bounce. Wool, nylon and Dacron are all used for the outer cover, hand-spun to ensure long wear and regulated fluffiness.

Traditionally, Europeans have favored a less lively ball that would last on the slow clay surfaces of the Continent. The Italian Pirelli ball, for example, seems absurd to Americans; it is impossible to serve an ace or to volley decisively with it, so inert is the ball's bounce. The Australians, English and Americans, known for their service and volley, cherish the fast, hard Slazenger ball used at Wimbledon, which gives special advantage to the power player. Recently, professionals have realized that the deader the bounce, the longer the rally and the happier the spectator. Since the spectator is responsible for their enormous prize money, tennis players have been agreeable to the spongier or pressureless ball. At the U.S. Open in 1970, without the players' knowledge, Tournament Director Bill Talbert used a clay-court ball, the tins of which he had opened beforehand so that the ball would be slowed down and the rallies further increased.

*The Major's Game of Lawn Tennis, a book by W. C. Wingfield, was part of a boxed set of distributed by Messrs. French and Company in 1873. Included were these "useful hints" for proper play and the diagram for the laying out of a court.*

If ball characteristics are ever standardized for international competition, the Tretorn ball of Swedish manufacture will have the best claim for acceptance. Its advertisements focus on its pressureless feature, demonstrated by an icepick puncturing the surface without changing the bounce. Inevitably, the trend will be to further slow down, or depressurize, the ball. It will make learning easier for beginners, and with the slower ball, players will get more exercise through longer rallies.

Like the rings of an old tree, the development of racquets has been an indication of the evolution of the game itself. Neither has progressed very quickly. However remarkable the changes in the racquet—an instrument that once was merely the palm of the hand—they have been painfully slow in coming. When callouses on bare palms were not

Above: *Herri met de Bles's* The Story of David and Bathsheba, *which shows tennis placed in even a biblical setting.* Right: *An early form of court tennis, a game still played by the wealthy in much the same form.*

considered protection enough, hands were wrapped in thick leather thongs. Later, padded gloves or mittens became fashionable, especially in handball, an early Irish offshoot of tennis. In the fourteenth century, the *battoir,* an instrument in the shape of a canoe paddle, appeared; it was later modified to a stubby-handled unit molded like a modern paddle-tennis bat. The wooden center area soon gave way to a primitive webbing of strings. Variations of racquet shapes were endless; some were triangles (base at the top), some olive-shaped, others round. Each variation was undoubtedly as much the result of damp weather and irregular handcrafting conditions as of preconceived design. The word *racquet* is of unknown origin, although there are credible attempts to trace it to the Arabic word *rahah* (meaning "palm of hand") or the medieval English word *rackle* (meaning "framework") or the Latin word *rec* (also meaning "framework").

The most popular misconception about racquets is that they are strung with catgut. The material popularly known as catgut is actually made from sheep intestines. The misnomer arose from the use of gut to string "kits," which are small violins of ancient origin; the transition from kitgut to catgut was understandable. Today, one 22-foot and one 11-foot length of separately twisted strands of sheep gut—the product of some 23 sheeps' innards—are required to string a single racquet. Over the years, there has been little im-

provement in stringing materials. Nylon, which is moistureproof and longer-lasting, is also less resilient than gut and is used primarily by lower echelon club players or children. Necessity may foster the development of new materials, for good-quality tournament gut is becoming scarce. Most of the world's gut supply comes from Australia and England and is hand-fabricated.

Old racquets were molded from a single strip of wood. Manufacturers discovered in the 1920s that separate pieces of wood glued together to form laminations strengthened the racquet, improved its beauty and reduced warping or breaking. It is an indication of the slow development of tennis that though there were no regulations controlling racquet size and weight, few experiments were made until recently to try new materials, shapes and sizes. A solid-steel bat with metal strings was considered a radical invention in the 1920s. But there was no imagination to its construction, and it was considered a clinker. In 1966, former Wimbledon and U.S. Champion René La-Coste came up with the first innovative design in the sport's history by fabricating a racquet out of tubular steel. Hardly anyone listened. The Wilson Sporting Goods Company bought a license to manufacture LaCoste's invention in America and persuaded Billie Jean King and Clark Graebner, as well as the author, to use the racquet at Forest Hills in 1967. King was an established star, and her winning the U.S. title with the Wilson "steelie" didn't raise an eyebrow. But Graebner's record had been unimposing, and the author was no longer a tournament player, merely a weekend performer. Graebner reached the finals; the author reached the semis. The metal-racquet rush was on. Every major manufacturer came out with a metal line. Spalding developed an aluminum model, Dunlop and Slazenger, a conventionally strung steel racquet with a tubular shaft. The Head Ski Company broke the market open with a sandwiched aluminum construction that retailed for $75. Such companies as Chemold, Sterling, Revere and Tensor, which had never made racquets before, recognized the natural offshoot of a metal-products business. Most of the subsequent experimentation on racquets has been with metal alloys or other base materials.

It shouldn't seem surprising that the average player is confused by the multiple choice of racquets that manufacturers have made available to

him. Bats of aluminum, plastic, steel, fiberglass, graphite and exotic combinations of all these have glutted the market. There is no such choice in golf. Ninety percent of all golf club shafts are made by one manufacturer. Golf club companies are, by and large, assemblers of parts only, and every company buys parts from the same source. The differences are cosmetic. But there are still no standards regulating the size of a tennis racquet. It can be as long as an oar and as wide as an umbrella. Inventors, therefore, have come up with designs both ugly and elegant.

Though there is freedom of equipment design, it has been accompanied by little latitude in the color and makeup of the tennis athlete's uniform. Until recently, uniforms had to be white. Arthur Ashe, perhaps ironically, led the charge to get color into the game. Forest Hills became the first major tournament to accept uniforms other than white, and stuffy Wimbledon is showing signs of breaking its restrictive white-uniform covenant. But typically, the change is coming erratically and with little logic. It is not unusual to see a professional wearing a blue shirt, white shorts, socks with red trim and grayish tennis shoes. Throw in a deep tan, and the player looks as put together as a gypsy on his day off.

Curiously, for a short time at the end of the nineteenth century, color was a part of the game. In 1881, Richard D. Sears won the first U.S. singles tournament at Newport over W. E. Glyn, 6–0, 6–3, 6–2. Though his triumph was convincing, Sears hardly looked like an athlete. He wore glasses, a colored blazer, long white trousers and a thin necktie. His style of dress was typical, perfectly suited to a leisurely style of play in which opponents stayed in the backcourt and patted the ball gently back and forth across the net. Doubles was played much more extensively than singles— the original court was laid out just for doubles, with no alley markings—and mixed doubles was a particularly popular game.

The original outfits for women's tennis would draw derisive hoots today. That players weren't expected to make sudden or speedy moves was probably a good thing. Flowing dresses buffered by elaborate slip arrangements, corsets and enormous hats with diaphanous veils were everyday wear for ladies in a mixed foursome.

Until not long ago, long flannel trousers for

Opposite: *A sixteenth-century French tennis player.*
Above: *The price list from Major Wingfield's book clearly depicts the equipment deemed necessary for a complete game.*

An Afternoon Bout at Tennis *by I. A. Abbey, painted in 1887.*

# RULES.

~~~~~

### I.

This Game can be played by two or four players.

### II.

The Game confifts of 15 aces, and the outfide have the option of fetting it, if they fhould happen to be 13 or 14 all, to either 3 to 5.

### III.

The fides having been made, and the one to go in having been determined on, as in Racquets, they place themfelves in court G, the firft player ftanding in the fervice creafe in the centre of the court, and ferves, which he does by throwing up the ball with his left hand into the air, and while falling ftriking it with his bat and fending it over the net

---

the men and longer dresses for the women were mandatory. In the early 1930s, Bunny Austin scandalized the game by introducing shorts in Britain, and there were unfeminine remarks when Alice Marble did the same in the United States a few years later. Lightweight tennis sneakers gradually replaced the cloddish street-shoe style of many years. Today every manufacturer has to make a leather track-type of shoe or else be run out of the market place.

There has been a repeated call to adopt a universal surface. This will probably never come about, if for no other reason than the obvious antitrust problem confronting an edict that all but one surface be banned. Clay has certainly replaced grass as the prestige surface, but one of the various synthetics with maintenance-free features will sooner or later become dominant. Like the racquet smorgasbord, there is an endless variety of rubber, plastic and artificial-carpet surfaces to choose from, but it is unlikely that any will quickly prove to be the dream surface, combining ideal bounce (slow and true), aesthetic qualities, low-maintenance cost and all-weather versatility. Perhaps the next vision will dictate an improvement of the

tennis shoe and ball to compensate for the shortcomings of the surfaces.

Until the 1970s, tennis was relatively ignored by spectators, who flocked to sports they considered more "masculine"—hockey, baseball and football. There was still thought to be something snobbish and effete about tennis; it had continued to be a rather leisurely pastime for rich WASPs (Arthur Ashe likes to point out that the term is redundant and should be ASP, there being no nonwhite Anglo-Saxon Protestants). There were, of course, a few understandable reasons for the image. No loud jeering, for example, is permitted to express a fan's disfavor at tennis matches, and neither spanking-white attire nor the word *love* are generally associated with such traits as ferocity and aggressiveness.

Too, the game suffered because some of its traditional elements seemed irrational. For instance, why the word *love* to signify no score? The French explain that their word *l'oeuf* means "egg." A duck egg in England and a goose egg in America both mean "zero." The Scots had a word *luff*, which also meant "zero." But whatever its derivation, the term *love* did not help erase the unfavorable image of tennis as a delicate, noncontact sport.

The scoring progression also seems irrational. Why 15, 30, 40? Attempts have been made to justify it with astrological work numbers and parallels with the 15-minute tolling segments of tower clocks, but to little avail. The old, sissy image of tennis is slowly breaking down, however. When a teen-ager reads that six tennis players each earned over $100,000 in 1972, those athletes gain respect and recognition not associated with the game a decade earlier.

There are now three nationally circulated tennis magazines, two of which compete on newsstands with a plethora of golf, football, hockey, basketball and baseball periodicals. At the end of 1972, the *New York Times* purchased *Tennis* from its publisher for a reported $350,000, and shortly afterward, CBS bought *World Tennis* for $2.5 million. The acquisitions spotlighted the spectacular financial growth of tennis. In addition, the tennis professional has been aided by the enhanced image of all athletes. A gifted sportsman is no longer beset by parents badgering him to give up frivolous games and settle down to a serious job. That once-frivolous game may now net the athlete more

## A LAY OF LAWN-TENNIS.

*By a Looker-On.*

Now, young people, the fine weather
    Will soon be gone.
Go and Tennis play together
    Upon the Lawn.
While the sun shines make your hay
    Between the showers.
Improve, like busy bees, to-day,
    The shining hours.
Time flies. For instance, look at me,
    And at your Aunt!
As you are now so once were we.
    But now we can't

Dance all night long till break of day,
    Nor, if we knew
How, at Lawn-Tennis could we play,
    Young folks, like you.
Already on the turf you tread
    The toadstool springs,
Which, when the Summer's drought has
    fled,
    Damp Autumn brings.
The grass will soon have got too wet;
    Too moist the mould.

Play whilst you can—don't play to get
    Your death of cold.
Play whilst those limbs you yet can
    use
    Free play allow,
Which they will by-and-by refuse;
    As mine do now.
Yet, on the sports of youth to gaze,
    One still enjoys;
As you may too, in future days,
    You, girls and boys.

---

SHAKSPEARIAN SAYING.

"THE man that hath no music in his soul," is a wretch who would not hesitate to buy a creaking boot.

HAPPY THOUGHT.

NAME FOR A NEW NEWSPAPER (*to be on the Breakfast Table every day*).—*The Morning Appetiser.*

---

Opposite: *Some of the rules from Major Wingfield's book that show the differences from and similarities to tennis as it is played today.*

Above: *The first tennis cartoon, published in* Punch *magazine.*

The Lawn Tennis Championship Match at Wimbledon *by Arthur Hopkins.*

Arthur Hopkins

Right and below: *Early twentieth-century women dressed for tennis with long, white skirts and large hats. Opposite: Tennis came to the stage. Shown is Louise Grudy as she appeared in* The Night Boat.

money in a season than the parents will earn in a lifetime.

The man credited with revolutionizing scoring in tennis is James H. Van Alen of Newport. Not surprisingly, Van Alen went about his task in a manner as confusing as the confusion he was trying to remedy. From 1957 to 1969, he experimented in his amateur and later professional tournaments at the Newport Casino with VASSS (Van Alen Simplified Scoring System) sets, which consisted of 31 points. He varied his systems every year in the consolation and first rounds. Players went berserk trying to remember what system they were laboring under. He ultimately devised the tie breaker

for games reaching 6-all, and the United States Lawn Tennis Association (USLTA) gave his system a trial period of exposure. Alastair B. Martin, president of the USLTA, persuaded the International Lawn Tennis Federation (ILTF) to allow the experiment at Forest Hills, and Wimbledon followed suit in 1971. Wimbledon's version, however, used a more conservative tie breaker (7 out of 12 points) that could last more than 12 points. The Forest Hills version was "sudden death" (5 out of 9 points); at 4-all in points, 1 point could decide the set. Professionals Gonzalez, Ashe and Newcombe disliked "sudden death," as it emphasized luck; spectators, however, liked it because it emphasized excitement. Van Alen's next crusade was to eliminate "love" and the 15, 30, 40 scoring progression, substituting 1, 2, 3; at 3-all, the next point would win the game. Sudden death would thus decide many, many games. He also wanted to change the name of Major Wingfield's game. "There are no lawns left," Van Alen pointed out. "It can't be lawn tennis anymore. Let's find another name."

It is not surprising, then, that when tennis started to shed its rich man's yoke, the stretching noises were like tiny explosions, tearing away at tradition and folklore. The principal casualty of these explosions has been the USLTA, the sport's governing body since 1881. Before that year, scoring systems varied, balls came in assorted sizes and some courts were hourglass in shape, whereas others had the eventually standardized rectangular design. The net sloped sharply from the net posts, and the height at the center strap varied from city to city. The USLTA was founded primarily to resolve these discrepancies and to provide organizational direction to a game that was headed everywhere and nowhere at once.

The USLTA, in its early efforts to maintain order, retarded the game's progress by failing to assist and coordinate the growth of professional tennis. Until 1968, over 99 percent of tennis crowds watched only the amateurs. All the best players were amateurs except a few barnstorming professionals, who each year played to small crowds that quickly lost interest in the one-night-stand format. Pro tennis, from the time of the first tour, promoted by Charles C. ("Cash and Carry") Pyle in 1925, was considered an outlaw activity and was excommunicated by the USLTA. When the great players

of the 1930s and 1940s—Bill Tilden, Fred Perry, Ellsworth Vines, Bobby Riggs, Don Budge and Jack Kramer—turned promoters, the USLTA looked away with the attitude of "that's not tennis; it doesn't concern us."

The association's prime delinquency was its failure to foster some form of open tennis. This failure allowed the ugly phenomenon of "Shamateurism" to fester for four decades. As the amateur game grew from 1920 to 1960, good athletes from all walks of life became top tournament players. Obviously, many of these men could not, in the tradition of Dick Sears, afford to pay their own way. In 1928, Bill Tilden wrote a number of articles for which he was paid and was therefore imme-

diately suspended by the USLTA. Ironically, the suspension was appealed by the French government to the U.S. State Department because Tilden, a tremendous gate attraction, was scheduled to appear in Paris for a Davis Cup Challenge Round. Tilden was reinstated.

In sports it has always been difficult to determine the point at which an amateur becomes a professional. For a long time, there was a stigma in being a pro, and slick accounting devices were used to preserve amateur status. Tennis went to extremes to keep the distinction. In 1934, a strict amateur code modified the rules to allow reasonable per diem expenses. The abuses were rampant. In 1967, the allowance reached $28 a day plus round-trip air fare. Enterprising players would schedule tournaments in two foreign cities near one another and collect overseas air tickets to both events. The $28 per diem allowance was intended for food and lodging that officials knew the player received free anyway. The tournament directors not only knew about the sham, they encouraged it. This conduct was condoned by the USLTA, which had strict amateur regulations, compared to those of other national associations whose players mocked top U.S. athletes for not asking for $1,000 a week. But the ILTF still failed to decree Shamateurism as professionalism. Pros were still so tainted that they were not allowed to play against amateurs. There was simply no open competition.

It took Wimbledon, the granddaddy of all tournaments, to revolutionize things in 1968, when the event was unilaterally declared open to all players. This was the event that "woke up" tennis. Other nations quickly followed suit, but two promoters, Dave Dixon and George MacCall, already had many players—including Rod Laver and John Newcombe—under contract, and they controlled the events their stars played in. As long as the fees requested by the promoters were modest, there was peace. Then Lamar Hunt, successor to MacCall and Dixon, stepped up his fees at Wimbledon in 1971, and then the trouble began. The ILTF banned contract pros from playing in events other than their own private promotions. All other tournaments, including the sacred Forest Hills, Wimbledon and Roland Garros events, continued to field independent pros (who maintained allegiance to

Opposite: *The evolution of the racquet* (left to right): *1874, 1875, 1878, 1879, 1880 and 1908.* Above: Lawn Tennis, *by St. John Harper and C. Weldon, practice at the Seventh Regiment Armory, New York, in 1881.*

national associations without contract) and amateurs, but they were stripped of many of the top names in tennis.

As usual, infighting by the rulers of sport resulted in catastrophe for the spectator. Peace was declared in July, 1972, after complex negotiations had resulted in Hunt's being given an exclusive time period every mid-January to mid-May to schedule his tournaments. In return, Hunt agreed not to sign any more players to contracts and to let existing contracts run their course. Hunt was thus left to promote his events with 64 of the world's best players in the winter and spring, and national associations vied to promote the summer events. An administrative power void in the sport was thereby created but was immediately filled by the Association of Tennis Professionals, whose concepts of change and control of the game made Hunt's look like child's play. The association had several aborted predecessors but now has gained the attention of every top professional. Its current

executive director, Jack Kramer, is not only one of the game's great champions but has invaluable experience as a pioneer promoter. The players, who for years could not muster enough strength to control their own destiny, suddenly have acquired power that is unprecedented for players in sports. In football or golf, the player associations started after the sports were functioning with solid management and administration. Not so in tennis. In 1968, after the first Open, when professional tennis flailed about looking for leadership but found no qualified takers, the Players Association interceded and now manages tournaments, controls rules, concludes TV contracts, as well as organizes the players themselves. The situation is unique and a trifle contradictory. The association is likely to be in a position to bargain with itself for better conditions.

Women's role in tennis is intriguing. Their position is difficult, but not as difficult as in golf, where women do not even compete in the same tourneys as men. Women tennis players are truly

Opposite: *Vanderbilt mansion indoor tennis court.*
Below: *Charlie Chaplin, Bill Tilden, Douglas Fairbanks, Mary Pickford,*
*Manuel Alonzo, Alex Weiner (Tilden protégé).*

appreciated in England, where dress styles are at least as important as an elegant backhand to the fashion-conscious English. In the U.S. women were once condescendingly accepted on the circuit and rarely with equal treatment. When appearance money was the method of paying participants, some top-ranked women players did not even collect enough to break even. Then, when extensive prize money was first offered, the ratio of purse distribution was as high as 12 to 1 favoring men. Wimbledon and U.S. champ Billie Jean King rebelled and, with the help of *World Tennis* editor Gladys Heldman, started a "women only" tour sponsored by Virginia Slims. The liberated women soon earned the group sobriquet of "women's lob," and their tour was an instant success. Spectators enjoyed the longer rallies inherent in the women's games. But even the power of women's lib did not give immunity from money problems, and soon the girls were threatened with suspension over a matter of sanction fees owed to the USLTA.

Mrs. Heldman is still the leader of the rebel group, now formally organized as the Women's International Tennis Federation. Its tour conflicts directly with the USLTA's schedule. Chris Evert and Evonne Goolagong were the only stars who refused to sign with Heldman, remaining instead within USLTA jurisdiction. While the seemingly endless wrangling continues unabated, one finds some satisfaction in that no one player or association has enough control to tyrannize minority interests of the game. Perhaps tennis, which for centuries ran without control, will never be tyrannized or fully tamed.

Tennis's thorny administrative problems, however, will never deter participant interest. Player strikes in baseball or football affect the popularity of those sports because they are spectator oriented. But because the bulk of tennis activity is concentrated among participants, strife at the top does not detract from enthusiasm for the game. Spectator enthusiasm has, however, verged on the fanatic.

The 1972 Davis Cup Challenge Round between the United States and Romania was supposed to foster international good will. Instead, it only increased nationalistic rivalries, many viewers treating it as a match of good against evil. The Romanian officials were suspected in many quarters of favoring the home team on line-calls, and Ion Tiriac was suspended for conniving to steal points from the Americans. An unnatural, jingoistic fever raged on both sides, destroying the supposed sporting nature of the contest. With the press and gallery exacerbating the rivalry, the match became almost a military campaign. Sport had vanished.

In recording the progress of modern tennis, two dates seem preeminent. One is 1968, when Britain decreed that Wimbledon would be open to professionals. The other is 1873, when Major Wingfield, the master innovator, combined three other racquet games, threw in a bouncy rubber ball for good measure and gave birth to the concoction "lawn tennis." Tennis had to wait a long time before its second step. The current explosion of interest is the pent-up energy from the many years of directionless, self-indulgent motion. But there is no reason for tennis to be embarrassed by its past, which, after all, is rich in history. The game suffered only because for so long it lived on its history alone. The elements of the sport itself, however, are so obviously appealing that tennis could not be restrained by its administrators any longer. Too, the recent concern for good health through exercise has given tennis prestige.

Tennis, with 11 million participants in America and 70 million throughout the world, will continue to flourish. Even the team-sport enthusiast must admit that it's fairly difficult for a football player after he's out of school—unless he's a pro—to call up two or three friends with the entreaty, "Come on over and we'll play a little tackle." But tennis is a true carry-over sport, a lifetime sport. And because of the small space needed to build a court, it will continue to capture the attention of town planners and developers with too limited an area in which to build a golf course.

The first Davis Cup match, in 1900, involved two Harvard boys and their social counterparts in England. Today's Cup matches draw entries from 60 nations, each fielding teams of unbelievable diversity. A Swiss prince, a Communist lieutenant, a steelworker's son, a French lothario, a South Afri-

can intellectual, a sheepherder's son and the descendant of a slave were participants in the 1972 competition.

The game's metamorphosis has been gradual but distinct. The rules of lawn tennis in 1873 stated that the purpose of the serve is "simply to put the ball into play." That concept has been radicalized more than any other element of the game. Instead of being used to commence a rally, the serve is now used to abort a rally. It is an instrument of destruction in its own right. Behind the savage sweep of his steel racquet, Wimbledon champion John Newcombe tries to win points instantly by the weight of his serve alone. The whole of modern tennis has undergone transformation almost as dramatic as the serve has. Major Wingfield would certainly have difficulty recognizing his game if he were to watch a match today.

Above: *In Central Park, New York, 1897.* Opposite top: *The first National Lawn Tennis Tournament, 1880, Staten Island, New York.* Opposite bottom: *The first Ladies Open Lawn Tennis Tournament, Staten Island, New York, 1883.*

3/
20 Aces

# Bill Tilden

Many, perhaps all of the greatest are here. It is the author's opinion that today's equipment, training methods and emphasis on and perfection of the serve and volley make today's players superior to those of the past. Furthermore, jet travel allows a player today to compete in many more tournaments. When Bill Tilden played Wimbledon, it was a nine-day ocean voyage to England. As recently as 10 years ago, the circuit was still a patchwork of competition. Today, the schedule jams events into every week of the year, and the players must train to be prepared for a match almost at a moment's notice.

We have not included as many women as men because, until recently, their contribution to the game has not been as great. Only now, as women players in general and Billie Jean King in particular raise their voices, are they beginning to gain the recognition they deserve.

Last, we have tried not to oversell the great players. They don't need it. Artificial praise cheapens rather than strengthens their fame. The old heroes in particular are susceptible to sentimental oversell, their weaknesses often blurred by nostalgia. To keep a balanced perspective, therefore, we have contrasted younger stars to their older counterparts, hoping that the comparisons will render a more precise picture of all the players' skills.

Bill Tilden singlehandedly elevated tennis to an attention level it was unaccustomed to. The Roaring Twenties embraced "Big Bill" as they did their other giants—Bobby Jones, Jack Dempsey, Red Grange, Gene Tunney and Babe Ruth. That Tilden alone could attract unheralded notice for himself and his then minor sport is indicative of his talents as a player and as a showman.

Bill was strictly box office. It was his standard fare to drop opening sets in a match so that he could stage a courageous if predictable comeback. He was tempestuous but not as today's stars are. He would not mope, curse or hurl his racquet. When unfairly favored by a call, he would toss the next point and bring the crowd to its feet. Nor was he above stalking a linesman after an errant call, regardless of whom it favored.

Tilden was the game's first professional before there was an organized pro game. While other players of his generation played part time and pursued business careers, Tilden's entire life was tennis. He studied the game, he practiced it relentlessly and he wrote about it. One of his books, *Match Play and the Spin of the Ball,* is still an accurate source book for experts and beginners.

In what would become a modern pro trend toward extended careers, Bill did not enter his prime until he was 27. That year (1920) he won the first of seven U.S. Championships and became the first American ever to win Wimbledon. After a career of epic matches against Bill Johnston, René LaCoste and Wilmer Allison, Tilden turned professional in 1931, at 38, though his aptitude for the sport qualified him for pro status a decade earlier when he was the master of amateur tennis.

*For 50 years Bill Tilden's name has been synonymous with excellence in every phase of tennis. Tilden had the style and balance of a dancer, the temperament of an actor and the savvy of a fight promoter.*

Tilden was an imposing theatrical figure. Six feet three inches tall and stoop-shouldered, he presented a gaunt rather than a dashing spectacle. He was a master of all the strokes and could impart topspin or underspin to all. He was not a server and volleyer in today's sense, though he probably could have been. He approached a rally as one would a buffet dinner, sampling a wide range of delights before concluding the ritual. The serve was a mere appetizer for the feast that followed. Any abridgement—a quickly closing ace, for example—would have been unfulfilling. As a result, none of Tilden's strokes impressed onlookers. He was a fine volleyer but only moved to net after the way had been carefully prepared by his groundstrokes. He never displayed great speed either at net or in the backcourt, though his long strides gave him mobility. Style was most important. He won six National doubles and a Wimbledon doubles, substantiating the argument that he was the game's complete master. In 1969, a panel of writers selected Tilden the greatest player of all time, a memorial to his impact on the game rather than an assertion that the old-timers could whip the moderns. As tennis was then played, Tilden, immaculate in long flannels and baggy cable-knit sweater, would surely have been undone by the faster tempo of today's game. But, like any virtuoso, he could have adapted to the modern style and excelled.

Tilden was tennis's first true professional. He devoted his life to increasing the game's popularity and extended his career well past his prime. Here, at 56, he plays Forest Hills.

# Helen Wills

Helen Wills earned her sobriquet, "Little Miss Poker Face," because she held all the aces. At 15, she already had the carriage of a champion. Even at this early age, unfazed by defeat and unimpressed by success, she concentrated intensely. Her style was as simple as her sailor-suit whites. She excelled at the baseline with booming groundstrokes that could keep opponents running endlessly in circles in the backcourt. She rarely tired and, though not quick on foot, she possessed stamina that made her steadfast and consistent. Adversaries wrestled with the dilemma of coming to net and being doomed by her precise groundstrokes or staying in backcourt and being exhausted.

Helen's serve was the hardest and fastest of its time, which had not yet adjusted to a woman athlete relying on force. Her weakness was at net, where her lack of agility made her suffer in rapid close-up exchanges. She recognized the weakness and maneuvered to avoid face-to-face confrontations at net.

Helen Wills focused attention on women's tennis for the first time. She ruled from 1920 to 1932, longer than any other woman champion, winning seven U.S. titles, eight Wimbledon Championships, four French Nationals and sixteen Wightman Cup triumphs, to compile the greatest collection of trophies in tennis history.

Her penetrating steel-blue eyes focused uncompromisingly on the task at hand. Only one defeat—to graceful Suzanne Lenglen at Cannes in 1926—marred her near-flawless international record. It was the most dramatic match in the history of women's tennis, more so because the two never met again. Perhaps, that dramatic defeat contributed more than any isolated triumph to her stature. Widely criticized for showing no emotion after either sensational wins or tragic losses, at Cannes she at least demonstrated some human fallibility, a trait many observers were not sure she possessed.

Helen Wills (later Helen Moody and Helen Roark) mastered tennis with endless practice, diligence and love. Unlike Tilden, Perry and Lenglen, she had no use for theatrics. She stuck to her mission with a single-mindedness that dismayed opponents. Her application of talent was unmatched —it was her life—and it is for this uncomplicated superiority that she is remembered.

*Even in those rare moments when caught off balance, Helen Wills was never flustered. "Little Miss Poker Face," whose trim sun visor characterizes her precision, established tennis's most enduring records.*

# Suzanne Lenglen

Even the most glorious legends fade. But the legend of Suzanne Lenglen survives untarnished, perhaps because it extends far beyond her considerable material accomplishments. She ruled the tennis world from 1919 to 1925, creating as many sensational headlines as her contemporary, Tilden. Comparing the two is inevitable. Both had an uncanny flair for the dramatic, but Mademoiselle Lenglen, with her doting mother always at her side, was as delicate as a tropical flower. In 1921, she came to Forest Hills after capturing Wimbledon for the third straight year and was everywhere acknowledged as number one. There were no seeds in those early years of the championships, which meant that she was at fate's mercy for her draw. Also, she had come to America overconfident and with little practice. It was Russian roulette, and in Molla Mallory, she drew the live cartridge, a human backboard with implacable will. Miss Mallory scorched the sensitive Lenglen, 6–2, in the first set, after which Suzanne developed a racking cough. With the score 3–0 against her in the second set, Lenglen defaulted in tears, claiming she was too sick to continue. It was one of the rare moments when her operatic outbursts did not enhance her game, the most glittering of any era.

Her long nose, crooked teeth and sallow skin seemed like mismatched puzzle pieces, but her grace and saucy charm gave her a majestic appearance. With racy midcalf-length dresses and bare

arms, she exposed more flesh than the corset-cinched spectators were used to, shocking the predominantly conservative spectators. A salmon-pink bandeau became her trademark. The colorful costumes caught on and became the forerunners of today's skimpy outfits, which place a premium on freedom of movement.

Lenglen's play matched her off-court grandeur. The accuracy of her groundstrokes menaced all opposition as she glided effortlessly from shot to shot. During her occasional forays to net, she would leap from side to side in high, ballerina kicks that would enthrall the gallery.

Her dramatic, triumphant confrontation in 1926 with Helen Wills at Cannes, France, after nearly two years buildup was the highlight of her career. To statisticians this single triumph does not compare with Lenglen's six Wimbledon crowns and six French Championships, but the classic elements of drama were present—vital elements to the flammable French lady.

So grand was the mystique that surrounded Mademoiselle Lenglen, that the legend persists that Lenglen never lost a match other than the default to Molla Mallory. She turned professional for the 1927 season and was the first crusader for women's pro tennis. But her life ended tragically. She died of a mysterious illness at 39. Suzanne Lenglen was true to her historic role to the end—glamorous, charismatic, enigmatic.

*Suzanne Lenglen added an artistic dimension to the sport's disciplined form and movement. Her angular, majestic style had the ease and grace of a ballet dancer's technique.*

# René LaCoste

In tennis the French Revolution didn't happen until 1924. It was worth the wait. Four Gallic stars, the "four musketeers," shone at the same time. Jean Borotra, "the Bounding Basque," was an extremely elegant stylist who led with his backhand and coveted a position close to the net. Henri Cochet was the child star with plumb-line precision in his groundstrokes, and Jacques Brugnon was the doubles expert. The unofficial D'Artagnan of the quartet was René LaCoste, the swashbuckling Parisian, the first man to surmount Bill Tilden's invincibility. LaCoste showed that his stunning form in the 1926 Challenge Round was no fluke, when in the following year he again triumphed over Tilden to lead the musketeers to a wild, surprise 3–2 win over the U.S. team. LaCoste was con-

vincing in both singles, beating Tilden again and beginning the six-year French stronghold on the sacred cup.

LaCoste was an enigma to defense. He seemed to know exactly what his opponent was thinking and where the ball would land long before it arrived. So great was his anticipation that he never gave the impression of hurrying. He always seemed to be waiting for the ball. His return of service was lethal, and his precise passing shots humiliated many a foe who jauntily advanced to the net without adequate preparation. LaCoste's court demeanor was as precise as his groundstrokes. His sombre mood frustrated French fans.

The sloe-eyed Frenchman won his native Nationals in 1925, 1927 and 1929. He toppled Jean

From left to right: *René LaCoste, unofficial D'Artagnan of the "four musketeers," makes a comeback in France, routs Bill Johnson in Philadelphia, takes Tilden at Wimbledon and anticipates perfectly a forehand volley.*

Borotra in 1926 in the only all-French final of the U.S. Championships and captured Wimbledon in 1925 and 1928. In LaCoste's epic matches with Tilden, his subtle intellect seemed to humble Big Bill's theatrical performances. In an era not yet fully aware of the potential of the big serve and volley, LaCoste used the serve as a guillotine. He laced Tilden with a profusion of aces and killing volleys, but his were weapons of surprise and cunning, not of power. Only when least expected would he serve and volley powerfully. His most respected talent was his mastery of the riposte. LaCoste had the answer to anything, and for three years Tilden was his perfect interrogator.

LaCoste excelled at anything he attempted.

When ill health struck in 1928, he became a respected force in business. Keeping a sharp eye on the game he cherished, he made the symbol of his playing days, the crocodile, a valuable and respected trademark on tennis clothes the world over. The current fuss over metal racquets is directly traceable to LaCoste's ingenuity. He licensed the Wilson Sporting Goods Company to manufacture a steel racquet of his design, and after the 1967 Forest Hills tournament, where his product met stunning success, the metal-frame bonanza was on. Despite his off-court success, René LaCoste will be most vividly remembered for his dedicated application to tennis and the wits, concentration and precision with which he played the game.

# Don Budge

Clockwise from top: *Budge takes 1938 Wimbledon title, lunges for a backhand and leaps net after first-round Forest Hills victory. Budge employed a pronounced swing that left little margin for error.*

With an ideal backhand, Don Budge ruled before prize money reached stratospheric heights and before lucrative endorsement contracts became commonplace. But 20 years after his peak, it was still more important to have his name on a racquet than the manufacturer's.

Tall and lean, with a clutch of red hair and freckles, Don Budge could have passed for Huck Finn. His record added to the all-American image. He won both the U.S. and Wimbledon Championships twice, in 1937 and 1938, and compiled an awesome 25–4 won–lost record in Davis Cup play. In his proudest accomplishment, he won the Sullivan Trophy, awarded to the nation's top athlete. He was the only tennis player to be so honored.

In 1938, his best year, Budge won the Aussie and French titles in addition to the U.S. and Wimbledon crowns—the sport's first Grand Slam. Three "slam tournaments" are played on grass, an advantage for power players and one that Budge exploited to the fullest. So devastating were his blasts, backhand and forehand, that he seldom rushed the net, though his upbringing on the slick cement courts of Oakland, California, had prepared him well for such an eventuality. On serve,

his lack of American twist or overspin for control required great confidence, for his slice skimmed perilously close to the net. Such confidence showed also in his volley, for which he employed a pronounced swing (rather than a more timid punch) that left little margin for error.

Budge dominated international tennis amid the festering politics that preceded World War II. In the late thirties, sport became political as world leaders used their star athletes to arouse their citizenry and to propagandize to the world. Don Budge carried the stars and stripes nobly in his matches with the German ace Baron Gottfried von Cramm, stirring sentiments far deeper than those of sport.

Budge turned professional for the 1939 season and after the war reestablished the preeminence of his bewildering backhand. More than any other player, he had the carriage of a champion. He walked with a gait that quietly exuded pride in his champion's stature. From his playing days, when his long flannels, cable-stitched sweaters and impeccably tailored shirts were his regal raiments, to his professional teaching days, no one in his presence doubted that he was a champion.

# Fred Perry

one of the game's most devastating shots. What began as a foe's attempt to exploit Perry's weak backhand, ended in an unsuccessful challenge to Perry's greatest strength. Perry recaptured Forest Hills in 1934 and in 1936. He won the French Championships in 1935 and the Australian Nationals in 1934, and he strung together nine Challenge Round singles and doubles victories with only one defeat. But his proudest record came in his native England, where the British don't consider a man a true champion until he has won "the Champion-

Fred Perry was as cocky as a Sunday rooster, and his talents matched his cocky strut. He was recognized as one of the most accomplished athletes tennis has produced. In the mid-1930s, when Perry was king, tennis was still considered a lawn party diversion reserved for the aristocratic upper crust. Some have explained that being the son of an artisan, Perry used arrogance as a defense. Worshiped by spectators everywhere, he seemed fascinated by his champion's mantle vanquishing the game's class distinction.

Perry's appearance was majestic—superior physique, jutting features, a saddle-brown tan and tailored white flannels. His early prowess in table tennis led him to a world championship and developed the agility, control and cunning that that game prizes. When Perry switched sports, his hand–eye reflex was readily adjustable to tennis, and his running forehand was directly traceable to the topspin wrist flick of his Ping-Pong days.

In 1933, the jaunty Briton paired with countryman Bunny Austin to break a six-year French stronghold on the Davis Cup. Perry reveled in his success, his jovial, outgoing manner a clear contrast to the traditionally English stiff-upper-lip image. On court, he would jest with ball boys. Off court, he sported a pipe, in mock concession to English propriety. But he could summon a rare single-mindedness to tennis—to the U.S. Nationals, for example, which he won in 1933. Perry's forehand flashed so effectively at Forest Hills that his backhand became suspect. But it did little good for a foe to probe there. Perry simply ran around the shot and parried on the forehand. Such a tactic would have left a normal player with the entire right court unprotected, but the Englishman compensated with a forehand hit on the run that was

*Replete in saddle-brown tan and tailored white flannels, Fred Perry runs through the Wimbledon field on his way to a record three consecutive titles.*

ships" twice. Perry did one better, winning Wimbledon successively in 1934, 1935, and 1936.

In 1936, Perry recorded his last amateur triumph when he squeezed by Don Budge in five sets at Forest Hills. Budge was younger and had been snapping at the Briton's heels for several years. At the U.S. Nationals it seemed that the Californian had caught Perry and was about to pass him. At 7–8 of the final set, Budge's blazing backhand had brought him to within two points of victory. But as so often in the past, a perilous position stirred Perry to produce his best tennis. With rapacious forehands and full-swinging volleys, he tore Budge like confetti to win his third U.S. title.

Budge was soon to reach his zenith, and Perry joined the touring professionals just in time to escape Budge's withering, triumphant quest for the Grand Slam in 1938. Perry played as a pro for eight years and immediately thereafter became one of the game's most active statesmen, writing a column for a London daily and contributing commentary to global radio and TV broadcasts.

# Bobby Riggs

In a world where bigger usually means better, Bobby Riggs was undersized and underrated. The 5-foot 8-inch Californian learned to discipline his shots on the fast cement of the Los Angeles Tennis Club. He accepted early in life that he could not overpower many opponents, so he carefully attended to keeping opponents from reaching the ball. Disgruntled big-game disciples could outhit but rarely outwit him. He was the master fox among the hounds. Riggs was so resilient on defense, and so precise with his groundstrokes that he rarely seemed to be on the defensive. Opponents scurried from corner to corner to retrieve his gentle, arching lobs.

He was known as a clutch player, whose competitive juices seemed to flow only when he was a service break or a set down. He was equally famous for his obsessive and not always friendly betting. If rain postponed his match, he would find a deck of cards and a hat and bet he could pitch more cards into the hat than his opponent. He could make a horse race of raindrops trickling down a window, betting which would reach the bottom first. Yet his playing style, if not his lifestyle, was model. His forehand and backhand were executed simply, without exaggerated loops or hitches, his overhead was uncannily accurate and he was never ashamed to lob.

Riggs's early success came from skill rather than brawn, but when he joined the professionals after the war, he added a firm volley and a more potent serve, and suddenly, the era's most famous baseliner had become an effective net rusher. Above all, Bobby Riggs had the mentality of a true professional. He could adapt to any strategy that would elicit his challenger's error.

Riggs won at Forest Hills in 1938 and 1940 and Wimbledon in 1939. As a pro, his most cherished victory was his triumph over Don Budge, 46 matches to 37, on their yearlong tour in 1947. His wins were built on simple principles—getting the first service deep into the corners and hitting the steady rather than the spectacular volley. He knew he could not trade crashing backhands with the heavies and, for a time, reverted to his retrieving forte, venturing to net only when his foe least expected him to. Perhaps, more than anything, his speed for short bursts helped him most. The rigors of a long tour are apt to produce sluggish play after a while but not from Riggs. He reached balls seemingly beyond reach.

Riggs was a champion of great guile. He assaulted opponents with a high-pitched chatter that must have sounded like squeaks to spectators. He launched an attack on the mind as well as on the body of his foe and rained confusion on both. He always liked his odds, regardless of the opponent. You can be sure that Riggs never bet against Riggs.

*Undersized at 5 feet 8 inches, Bobby Riggs could be outhit but never outfoxed. Riggs was best under fire, as at Wimbledon (opposite) in 1939, when he won the championship with groundstrokes and precise lobs.*

# Pancho Gonzalez

At 44, Pancho Gonzalez is not content to be a legend. In 1970, he surprised Rod Laver at his peak, in the Howard Hughes Open, 6–1, 7–5, 5–7, 6–3 and, in 1971, won the Pacific Southwest over a field that included Cliff Richey, Jim Connors and Stan Smith. As recently as December, 1972, he won $10,000 in less than two weeks. He reached the finals of the $75,000 Clean Air Tennis Classic, losing only narrowly to fellow American Charlie Pasarell. Four days later he beat Clark Graebner in the finals of the Rothman's Spectacular in Jamaica. This championship performance came from a man who has retired annually for the last 12 years.

Gonzalez's record during his most vibrant years is difficult to measure. He won the U.S. Nationals in 1948 and 1949 and won two stunning singles victories in the 1949 Challenge Round against Australia. Then, at 21, he quit the amateur game when he was its premier player. But the professional game at the time had room for only one winner. After Jack Kramer drubbed him on his initial pro tour in 1950, Gonzalez had to wait for three years, while Kramer destroyed Pancho Segura and Frank Sedgman. Gonzalez surfaced briefly in 1953 to win the U.S. professional title, one of the few tournaments that he could enter. He was a champ with no place to play because pro tennis could not then support full-scale tournaments, and open tennis would not come until 1968. Then, in 1954, Kramer, the tour's new operator, signed Gonzalez again. For a decade he ruled world professional tennis. He won the U.S. pro title a record eight times, crushing many a glittering reputation built

*Pancho Gonzalez was king of the court, whether playing Wimbledon in 1949, where he was upset (above), or playing Forest Hills 22 years later when he teamed with his son in the championships (opposite).*

*Gonzalez never received instruction yet displayed
perfect form. His serve, perhaps his most famous stroke,
was the perfect amalgam of power and grace.*

in the amateur ranks. Pancho sent all the stars home nursing their bruised pride: first Sedgman and Segura, then in succession, Tony Trabert, Ken Rosewall, Lew Hoad and Rod Laver.

Gonzalez was, perhaps, the most gifted player who ever lived. He never received tennis instruction. His superior talent caught the eye of California officials, who provided the top competition he needed to refine his primitive style. When Gonzalez quit school in the tenth grade, officialdom

barred him from all junior tournaments. Gonzalez sharpened his mighty skills from competitiveness alone. Soon truancy was behind him, the road to legend ahead.

It is not easy to say which of Gonzalez's assortment of weapons contributed most to his success. True, his serve was the perfect amalgam of power and grace and crucial to his brilliance. The importance of other factors is less obvious. Certainly, he was the game's most bitter and effective com-

petitor. He surrendered no match until the hand-shaking ceremony at the end, and sometimes not even then. In addition, he was the only player to combine a brutal offense with a dedication to defense, when the situation demanded it. It was a familiar sight to see him charging from corner to corner, throwing up high lobs or chipping deep to regain court position. At 6 feet 2 inches and 180 pounds, Gonzalez was a large man yet supernaturally mobile. He was a panther, crouched low, stalking every ball with an animal's hunger, searching for the kill. His moves covered sizable expanses without appearing to, while fleeter runners looked strained and tense.

The majesty of Gonzalez will always be with us. His dynamic serve will forever be his legacy, but one has to search his soul to uncover his formula for triumph. Perhaps, he is reluctant to pass on such secrets, fully aware by now that after every retirement there may be a comeback.

# Jack Kramer

No one has had a greater influence on the tennis world than Jack Kramer. He ruled first as a player, then as a promoter and finally as the executive director of the powerful Association of Tennis Professionals. He was a perfectionist in each role.

Everyone rates him among the five all-time great players, unusual perhaps, because his statistical success was not on a par with Tilden's, Budge's, Laver's and Perry's. But in a short time he created a lasting impression. As an amateur, he won Forest Hills in 1946 and 1947 and captured Wimbledon in 1947. In the same years, he spearheaded two U.S. Challenge Round victories over Australia. But Jack Kramer was a practical man. Not content with repeating his glorious amateur triumphs, he succumbed to the challenge of Bobby Riggs and the pro tour in 1948. Kramer battered Riggs, 69 matches to 20. In 1949, Gonzalez, the world's amateur champion, challenged the new professional king. Kramer pulverized Gonzalez, 96 matches to 27, and after making quick work of Pancho Segura the next year, 64–28, Kramer took the promotional reins of the tour from Bobby Riggs. He was as successful a promoter as he had been a player. He terrified every national tennis association by luring entire Davis Cup teams away from the amateur ranks with lavish pro contracts. His brilliant, ever-increasing crew of barnstorming athletes attracted other entrepreneurs, who continued the business Kramer had devel-

*Among Kramer's titles are the 1947 Wimbledon* (opposite top), *where
he beat Tom Brown, and the 1946 United States Championships*
(opposite bottom and below), *where he again beat
Tom Brown. Rated among the five all-time great players,
Kramer has had more influence on tennis than anybody else.*

oped, and eventually forced open tennis with the
sheer number of players who had over the years
abandoned the amateur game.

Kramer's playing style was similar to his promoter's style—straightforward attack. He mastered
the "big game" of the forceful serve and killing
volley. Many before Kramer followed a big serve
to net, but none relied on this tactic so heavily or
with such calculating precision. Kramer's relentless
charge to the net was a distant cry from the occasional forays of his predecessors. Jack was the first
to understand that the core of the attack is the
accuracy of the first serve, which can instantly put
the receiver on the defensive. His volley was heavy
and sure. His forehand was the master stroke he
relied on to break serve. At 6 feet 1 inch and 175
pounds, Kramer had the perfect build for a tennis
star, and though not as athletic as McKinley, Nastase or Perry, he drilled himself with such diligence that his serve and forehand were acknowledged as two of the most mechanically faultless
strokes in the game.

Kramer has excelled in different phases of
tennis when each was the controlling element in
the game. Now he leads a powerful players' association, which, despite its weak predecessors, is
certain to become more influential than either national associations or the International Lawn Tennis Federation. Once again, Jack Kramer's "big
game" rules the sport.

# Tony Trabert

Through the years, tennis has suffered because football, basketball and baseball were quicker to attract natural, flamboyant young athletes. Never did tennis receive a more glamorous boost than with the arrival of Tony Trabert. He was the all-American boy, with crew cut, the rocky frame of a halfback and the electric grin of a rock star. By the time he was six, the public courts of Cincinnati were his private playground. But the Cincinnati kid was not a one-sport specialist. His broad, sturdy back, cannonball legs and smooth versatility made him a stickout basketball starter for the University of Cincinnati.

Trabert's sports career was channeled to tennis by fellow Ohioan Bill Talbert. Talbert nurtured his protégé, and in 1950, when Trabert was only 19, the pair won a number of successive doubles matches, including the Italian and French Nationals. When only 21, while an ensign in the navy, Trabert gave Forest Hills champion Frank Sedgman his toughest battle in that tournament, before losing narrowly in five sets in the semifinals. The performance sent Trabert rising meteorically to third place in the U.S. rankings.

A two-year tour in the navy stifled Trabert until 1953, when he charged from the service to the center court at Forest Hills and captured the Nationals over Vic Seixas in a sensational straight-set final. In the 1953 Davis Cup, he lost a titanic struggle to the talented Australian firebrand, Lew Hoad. Unable to exit coolly after having been favored to win, Trabert excoriated the Aussie crowd for having cheered his double faults. But at the Davis Cup showdown the next year, he withered wonder boy Hoad with a blinding array of serves and volley winners. After sweeping the fourth set

(6–2, to win the match) and after teaming with Seixas to recapture the Davis Cup, Tony apologized to the crowd for his fiery talk the year before. Applause rained down as Trabert's grin seemed to stretch across the sunset. Trabert never had to apologize again. In 1955, he was the champion of the world, capturing the Wimbledon, the U.S. and French Championships, the U.S. Indoors and the U.S. Clay Courts. Never before had anyone shown such virtuosity on as wide a variety of surfaces.

Trabert's style was as free and as forthright as his character. His size disguised his speed. A big, sturdy player can hit with more power than his more frail counterpart but usually surrenders part of his advantage because he lacks speed. Trabert surrendered nothing. He could serve fireworks, explode groundstrokes and yet move to remote court positions with graceful ease. His backhand was near perfect, never defensive and with a slight topspin that terrorized net-rushing opponents. Trabert's follow-through carried him further than others to the center of the court, in preparation for an offensive. His physical attributes added to his sound tactical sense could torment opponents. There seemed to be no weaknesses. Even his sportsmanship discouraged foes, for they realized that a Trabert victory would be a popular one.

When he turned professional at the end of 1955, Trabert was unhappily matched against Pancho Gonzalez at his leanest and meanest. Trabert lost the overall tour but kept Gonzalez constantly aware that a revitalized Trabert could quickly reverse the series. In 1970, Tony Trabert was elected to the National Lawn Tennis Hall of Fame, an obvious honor for the Cincinnati kid who added so abundantly and ebulliently to the game.

75

# Roy Emerson

It is ironic but not surprising that selecting Roy Emerson among 20 of the all-time best will raise more than casual skepticism. But on his record alone, he is more deserving than any modern player save Laver. He holds a record six Australian titles, two U.S. Championships, two Wimbledons and two French singles. His Davis Cup record is unbelievable—he lost but one singles match in 10 years of Davis Cup play. In doubles, Laver considers him the finest in the world. Roy has the titles to prove it, having won two Italian doubles, a Canadian, three Wimbledons, six French and four U.S. titles.

His image suffers because he excelled as an amateur when the pros scorned the amateur caliber. Emerson did not succumb to the lure of a professional contract until 1968, perhaps because, as he is the first to admit, his days as an "amateur" were quite profitable. Even so, at his prime, tennis was not yet big business, which prevented him from cashing in on the bounty that lesser talents soon shared. His primary skills, power and speed, had waned by the time he turned pro. "Emmo" can still produce his lightning form of the mid-1960s but cannot sustain the brilliance long enough to capture a major title.

While endorsement contracts and appearance fees are negotiated by more assertive and less able pros who inflate their modest skills, Emerson remains reticent. But his aggressive play contrasts markedly with the quiet business demeanor. His athletic ability and his concern for physical fitness make him a unique competitor. Stories proliferate of his running, not jogging, four miles around a lake after every match at the National doubles in Boston and jumping the hedge at the Meadow Club in Southhampton during his roadwork. (The hedge is five feet high and three feet deep.)

Critics contend that he can't vary his pace when he starts to lose. The weakness is more of style than of mind, traceable to his bold strokes, with no topspin at all for control. In good form, Emerson is a streak, but even on an off-day, his fitness and speed usually keep him in control.

Despite his quiet manner, Emerson has always been a leader. Young players have tried to emulate his three-cadence windup on serve, and his aggressive backhand "pop" off return of service is the envy of every professional. Even grizzled veteran Pancho Gonzalez has learned one of Emmo's tricks—cutting out the pockets of one's tennis shorts to make them lighter. Off court, Emerson shines as a simple, honest companion. He may be overlooked in history but never by his fellow pros.

*Emerson in action at Forest Hills
(above and left) and Madison Square
Garden (top). His record is
unbelievable—six Australian titles,
two United States, two Wimbledon, two
French and one loss in 10 years
of Davis Cup competition.*

# Maureen Connolly

Maureen the Magnificent performed her miracles quickly, before Fate became the only opponent to foil her mighty groundstrokes; at the height of her career, she suffered a crippling leg injury while horseback riding. Still, in four years she accomplished more than most stars do in a lifetime. From 1951 to 1954, she won nine major championships, including two French, one Australian, three Wimbledon, and three U.S. titles. During that time she was beaten only once—by Beverly Fleitz in California in 1954.

Maureen won Forest Hills at 16, an unbelievably young age at which to triumph over the collective experience of rivals Doris Hart, Shirley Fry, Louise Brough, and Margaret Dupont. At age 18, she became the first woman to capture the Grand Slam, and that same year, 1954, she achieved for the third successive time the Associated Press poll award as the woman athlete of the year.

"Little Mo" was trained on the sure, fast cement courts of her hometown San Diego, yet she never learned the violent serve and volley of the modern net rushers. She didn't have to. Her barrage of basic ground fire rarely required a concluding volley. In this regard Maureen is often compared to Chris Evert, the current *wunderkind*, who relies almost exclusively on a precision forehand and a two-fisted backhand. Like Evert, Connolly thrived on Zen-like concentration and rarely explored the area around the net unless lured there. But unlike Chris, who arrived on the tennis scene unheralded and with little expected of her at first besides a twinkle in her eye and pompons on her sneakers, Maureen was expected to excel at 16. The women players eagerly trained their sights on the young Californian, and the press relentlessly pressured her. She frequently found herself in early-round danger against opponents of modest skills. Chris is the sport's Cinderella, the subject of a gentle myth that fans really never want dispelled. But Maureen shines on merit alone.

Businesslike and relentlessly determined on court, Maureen used her speed as more than just a casual asset. It is hard to forget the sight of her streaking cross-court to unleash a steaming forehand.

Her triumphs came in such a cluster that it is difficult to isolate her most memorable one. Perhaps her victory over Doris Hart in the '52 Wimbledon deserves top billing. Top-seeded Hart and second-seeded Connolly both annihilated semifinal foes before they met—a match between the two best women players in the world. Miss Hart was more accomplished and more experienced than her younger rival, and her varied strokes stymied Connolly's rhythm, but Maureen prevailed, 8–6, 7–5, unruffled to the end.

Connolly achieved her matchless sequence of nine world titles before she reached the age of 20. It was surely only a prelude to what she might have accomplished with five more years of playing time.

In a career drastically foreshortened by injury,
"Little Mo" managed to win nine world
titles before she reached the age of 20.
Perhaps her most satisfying win came
against Doris Hart at Wimbledon in 1952.

# Rod Laver

Australian Rod Laver brought space-age enormity to tennis. Never before has a player dominated tennis so thoroughly and won more money doing it. His supremacy has lasted for more than 10 years, beginning in 1960 with the first of three Australian titles. Though slight, at 5 feet 8 inches and 160 pounds, he has the strongest left wrist in tennis, a wrist that makes his other arm look underdeveloped. His game is based on whippy groundstrokes, both forehand and backhand. His steel wrist produces enormous topspin, which bewilders net rushers. Laver's backhand compares to the mighty Don Budge's, the ultimate praise, but the similarity to Budge does not stop there. Both possess a flaming crop of red hair. Both are the only men to have captured the Grand Slam. After Laver's Slam in 1962, he joined the pro ranks to cash in, finally, on talent that amateur tennis rewarded with only "under the table" expenses, lucrative, to be sure, but pin money compared to the purses that were soon to come.

Laver has won two French, two U.S. titles and four Wimbledons, a modern record. But his most amazing feat was his triumph in the 1971 Tennis Champions Classic. Each of the early matches was a $10,000 winner-take-all match. He was invincible, winning 13 straight matches and a breathtaking $160,000. His narrowest escape was against Tony Roche, who held match point in the fourth set, only to fall victim to a miraculous comeback, a Laver trademark. Laver's final victory, over Tom Okker, was worth $35,000. The loot was in the bank before the middle of May, a prosperous beginning to any season. But "the Rocket" was not finished. By the end of the year, he had pocketed $292,717, a record for the sport (and more, interestingly, than the $241,872 won by golf's number-one winner, Jack Nicklaus). Laver became the first tennis player to earn $1 million, which he collected over nine years.

Laver's incredible winnings may be matched, but two of his contributions will not be. Before 1969, only Budge besides Laver had won a single Slam. In 1969, Laver had his second. His primary legacy, however, will be his style. Before Laver, the vicious topspin forehand had been used only as an experiment or a bizarre change of pace. The fleet Aussie developed it into a potent weapon. Laver similarly revolutionized the backhand. In prior years, most pros had reverted to the strategy of chipping deep and low to the backhand and rushing the net. First to be probed in any tight match, the backhand takes more preparation than the forehand, and its direction is easier to predict. Laver responded to this strategy by imparting so much spin to his backhand that the ball dipped at the net rusher's feet. Today, every player has been influenced by Laver's technique, and many, including Santana, Okker and Nastase, improvise with heavy topspin on forehand and backhand.

Like so many Australians, Laver's composure on court is unshakeable. No matter what the pressure, he remains tranquil. His superior stroking power, complemented by fleetness not often credited him, makes him win, reason enough for any athlete to be tranquil.

*Never has a player dominated tennis so thoroughly and won more money doing it than has Rod Laver. His steel wrist allows him to hit with devastating topspin, a fact that has made the Rocket more than $1 million.*

# Arthur Ashe

Arthur Ashe, nicknamed "the Shadow" by his Davis Cup teammates for his silent, flitting movements, was the first black man to succeed at tennis. Althea Gibson's credentials were better than Ashe's (two Wimbledon and two U.S. titles), but her glory came too soon—before the big money.

Ashe's first serve is unpredictable in direction and fast, impossible to anticipate and difficult to return. He hits a volley farther in front of him than any other player, keeping opponents off balance. He has faultless concentration and is utterly unflappable—"Icey Ashe" to the nicknamers. But his weaknesses are evident. He doesn't bend his knees on a volley, he doesn't dig for retrieves and he has a relatively weak second serve. Ironically, his greatest weakness was an outgrowth of his great talent, according to fellow pros. His natural racquet talent gave him so many options that he was likely to choose the wrong one. Pancho Gonzalez, in awe of Ashe's virtuosity, once said, "If Ashe would ever limit his backhands from ten varieties to three he would be the best player alive."

With superb timing and balance, Ashe overcame his shot-selection problem by hitting hard uncompromisingly. When his timing is slightly off, he will still lose but only to a great player. In 1965, his timing was rarely off when he scored three of his most impressive, but least heralded triumphs, at Melbourne, Brisbane and Adelaide. He crushed Australian stars Newcombe, Stolle and Emerson when the Aussies seemed invincible. In 1968, he won the first Madison Square Garden Open, took the U.S. Amateur and U.S. Open titles and won a critical Challenge Round Davis Cup singles match against Australia, compiling a winning streak of 26 matches.

*Arthur Ashe, "the Shadow," was the first black man to succeed at tennis. His power is legendary, his variety of shots endless. Gonzalez claims that Ashe has the potential to become the best player alive.*

Ashe's play sputtered from 1968 to 1972 because, many believed, he had other things on his mind, particularly, defining his responsibilities to his race. He worked vigorously to become the first black tennis player ever to visit South Africa, and his pioneering efforts succeeded, in a sense, although another black was granted the first visa. Despite his political diversions, Ashe is always ranked among the four top players in the world, with Laver, Rosewall and Newcombe. But because he often shows his brilliance in less prestigious tournaments, the public has erroneously thought he is past his prime.

Ashe's style is unabandoned attack. He wields his racquet as effortlessly as one might flick a fly swatter—none of the plodding racquet work of a clay courter who tries to keep the ball on the racquet face longer to add control. In his playing as in his life, Ashe is casually precise. He is distinctively modern.

# John Newcombe

John Newcombe is the prototype of the modern power player. Blessed with the perfect tennis build —sturdy legs, sleek torso and broad shoulders— he relies heavily on serve and volley. Newcombe is not one to prolong the rally. There may be other players who have the same philosophy, but they lack the physical prowess to execute in similarly brutal fashion.

Newcombe was raised on the quick pitch of White City Stadium's grass courts in Sydney, Australia. Under the wise tutelage of Davis Cup captain Harry Hopman, Newcombe was given his first Challenge Round singles assignment when only 19 years old. He lost to the more experienced players McKinley and Ralston, but he never lost his ambition of becoming the world's number-one player. He didn't wait long. In 1967, he won both Wimbledon and Forest Hills and emerged as the game's top amateur.

Newcombe was one of many tossed in the sea of confusion before the game was opened to professionals in 1968. With a pair of 1967 titles, he considered himself the best player, pro or amateur, and few disagreed. To prove the point, he turned professional at the beginning of 1968 and, by 1971, had cornered two more Wimbledon singles victories. The scribes finally agreed with Newcombe and voted him the best player of 1971.

The phenomenal Aussie's simple style, devoid

*John Newcombe displays his power at Las Vegas* (above) *and at Forest Hills* (opposite). *Newcombe has won three Wimbledon titles, and his heavy serve and volley garnered him Player of the Year award in 1971.*

of subtlety or guile, is uncompromising force. Newcombe's serve is devastating. Its motion carries him to within a few feet of the net for the first volley. His first and second serves are identical—both sliced severely. Such serving puts safety at a minimum but carries a deeper thrust, preventing a foe from taking the offensive. His forehand is a scimitar, dispatching all but the boldest returns. His backhand is less punishing, but rarely do rallies last long enough for his opponent to probe his weaker side. Only when a defender finds his backhand does John chip the return and wait for a chance to use his crushing forehand again.

In the tradition of Australian sportsmen, Newcombe is rarely upset at a poor line-call or a lucky let-cord. His composure bolstered by his confidence, he keeps his crashing strokes accurate. At 28, Newcombe is still an extremely young champion. As he sets the example for junior players who want to succeed with a limited repertoire of straight-ahead power strokes, it will be interesting to note the durability of the approach. John will never extend his elite career by reverting to touch and deception, like aging Ken Rosewall. True, the extraordinary prize money in tennis has already encouraged players to survive and prosper into the mid-30s, when a decade earlier athletes had no incentive to last past 30. But how long can a power player endure? John Newcombe, if anyone, can push the limit toward middle age.

# Ken Rosewall

It is rumored not unreliably that Ken Rosewall still has his first sixpence. For almost 10 years, he worked diligently but with little recognition and just as little compensation as the world's number-one or two professional. In 1968, open tennis became a reality, but Ken was already 33, and the consensus was that his glory had passed. Unconvinced at 35, he won the U.S. Open Championships (1970), and at 36, he won the World Championship of Tennis in Dallas, over Rod Laver. That triumph alone earned him $50,000. Finally, in 1972, at a spritely 37, he repeated his WCT triumph, again over Laver, for another $50,000. Many claim it was the finest match in tennis history.

Throughout his career, Rosewall's performances have startled the experts. The 5-foot 8-inch, 145-pound Australian was considered too small to excel on grass, yet (at only 18) he won the Australian Championships. The same year, he won the French Championships and, with Lew Hoad, won the Australian, French and Wimbledon doubles crowns. The connoisseurs were baffled; no one had ever dominated doubles with such a modest serve. The secret, of course, lay in the terrorizing volley that followed his serve. His footwork is so quick that he can reach passing shots with a nimble fencer's lunge. His forearm strength is deceptively great, particularly on balls hit at his midsection.

Despite his incredible record compiled as a youngster, his modest and quiet manner kept him inconspicuous. First, his more dynamic teammate, Lew Hoad, overshadowed him. Then, Gonzalez tamed Rosewall in his first pro tour, further obscuring him. Even when Gonzalez entered the first of his many retirements, in 1960, Rosewall's three-year reign as professional champion awarded him little recognition. In 1963, Rod Laver arrived. Though both Gonzalez and Rosewall took turns beating Laver, the public seemed always to consider the defeats an upset. At the first open tournament, in 1968, at Bournemouth, England, Mark Cox, an amateur, surprised established pros Gonzalez and Emerson, but few recall that Rosewall won the event. Then, three weeks later, Rosewall won the French Championships, 15 years after his first triumph there. When he recaptured the Aussie Open in 1971 and 1972, titles he had first won years earlier when he was 18, he set the bizarre record of having had the longest period between championships in a major event.

His style is confounding. While others relentlessly pound their serves and contort their wrists to add more topspin to the backhand, Rosewall plods along with a steady pop-it-in serve and a slice backhand. But that underspin backhand with the precision of a suture is considered the equal of Budge's and Laver's. For a pro, playing Laver is relatively painless, even while losing, because Laver's shots zoom to distant sectors of the court allowing no chance for retrieve. But against Rosewall, a rally is punishing. His groundstrokes penetrate deep, from side to side, but leave hope for a gallant return. His rival makes a heroic lunge, only to be sent wearily pursuing Rosewall's next riposte.

Whether or not Rosewall receives the attention due him, his devastating backhand will continue to punish older and younger foes alike.

*Ken Rosewall won his first major championship at 18 when he took the Australian; 19 years later he won his second WCT championship over Rod Laver. At 38, Rosewall looks hopefully to a Wimbledon title.*

# Stan Smith

At 26, Stan Smith has accomplished a great deal in tennis against history's better players and with more at stake. He began playing at 16, a late age by championship standards, and was junior champion two years later. The story persists that Smith was rejected as a ball boy because he was too awkward. He still doesn't move like a natural athlete, but hard work, courage, concentration, discipline and forthrightness are potent substitutes. Add a gargantuan reach and a powerful serve and volley and one has an awesome arsenal.

Tennis does not often reward creativity. The man who can master the prosaic may be unexciting, but he is usually successful. Such is the case with Stan Smith. He won the U.S. Open in 1971, Wimbledon in 1972, the Grand Prix in 1971 and every Davis Cup singles match he has played. He wins when least expected. The best example was two straight-set victories over Ilie Nastase on clay when the Challenge Round outcome was in doubt.

Stan's emotional range is limited, but this too

*Like John Newcombe, Stan Smith relies on the serve and the volley. Smith won the 1971 U.S. Open and the 1972 Wimbledon and has never lost a Davis Cup match.*

assists him. There are no theatrical binges to side-track his mission. His style is artless, but an element of craft has crept into Stan's game. He uses an occasional dropshot, a lob and a change of pace on groundstrokes, not enough to deceive but enough to frustrate an opponent accustomed to his usually predictable if not pleasant barrage.

Smith is deeply religious. He has little time for humor, so altruistic are his commitments and so constant his introspection. His game is a reflection of his personality—honest and straightforward. His serve is typically direct—straight windup, high toss, vicious downswing. His long legs give him mobility not associated with a big man. Stan's volley is conventional and crisp, but his exceptional reach makes him impossible to pass. Height and reach give him a formidable overhead. He adds enough topspin to both forehand and backhand to reinforce his attack. No one else has applied basic weapons so judiciously. Stan Smith wins with simple truths.

# Margaret Court

Like guns mounted on a battleship, Margaret Court's searing service and flashing forehands are founded on superb and, for women's tennis, unique physical fitness and strength. Margaret trained heartily on roadwork, weights and other previously all-male techniques in former Wimbledon champion Frank Sedgman's gymnasium in Sydney. Her physical prowess is Amazonian; she has strong hands, broad shoulders and sinewy, slender legs. At 5 feet 10 inches, Margaret serves bullets while her counterparts gently poke their deliveries in court. She has won more major titles than any other player. Her most astounding record is winning the Australian Nationals 10 times, a mark not likely to be equaled. Mrs. Court has also won three French titles, three Wimbledons and four U.S. Championships.

Her power comes not only from her dedication to regimented gym workouts but also from regular sparring sessions with countrymen Roy Emerson and Fred Stolle. Even these men marvel at Margaret's might. Less assertive off the court, she has kept her publicity to mortal proportions with unassuming modesty. She has also taken time out from the tour to have a child.

Occasionally, even Margaret suffers from the frayed nerves that plague weekend players reg-

*Margaret Court is physical prowess personified.*
*She has won more major titles than any other player, including*
*an incredible 10 Australian championships.*

ularly. More than once Billie Jean King has stolen the offensive in their matches, and the surprise of someone copying her hurricane attack occasionally befuddles Mrs. Court. But she has won what King never has—the Grand Slam. In 1970, Margaret Court sailed through the Australian, French, Wimbledon and U.S. titles, a feat accomplished only once before by a woman, in 1953 by Maureen Connolly.

Margaret's phenomenal physical stature has intimidated foes for over a decade, but now, rather than surrendering in awe, opponents have overcome the fear of losing their femininity if they emphasize force rather than grace. Whether or not others approach her imposing record of major championships, Margaret Court will be remembered as the first woman to employ the Spartan training regimen of the men. That is the bulwark of her strength, stamina and speed. Margaret is indestructible.

# Evert and Goolagong

The nineteenth ace is two people: Chris Evert and
Evonne Goolagong. Were neither to lift a racquet
again, they would deserve places of honor because
of their invigorating impact on the game in two
short years. Goolagong, combining a blithe spirit
and a rhapsodic style, won the French Championships in 1971. Apparently taken by her aboriginal
ancestry as well as by her tennis proficiency, European magazines splashed her picture on their covers. Never had a woman player stirred such a fuss.
A month later, she won Wimbledon, disposing of
Billie Jean King in the semis, 6–4, 6–4, and Margaret
Court in the finals, 6–4, 6–1. Only 19, she had
added a wild sparkle to the dull women's tour.

Two months later, tennis had a second Cinderella—16-year-old Chris Evert. Chris contributed
two vital wins to America's 4–3 Wightman Cup
victory over England. A week later, she won the
Eastern Grass Court Championships, startling the
experts, who expected her downfall on a fast surface. Then she brought her miracle parade to
Forest Hills. In the second round, she survived six
match points to win, 6–1, in the third set. She followed with two come-from-behind, three-set victories over Françoise Durr and Lesley Hunt. Suddenly, she was in the semifinals against Billie Jean
King, and the world was watching—15 news crews,
more than for any other sporting event in New
York. But even Cinderella had to go home. Chris
lost to King, the ultimate champion, 6–3, 6–2.

But the week was still Chris's. Later she ap-

*Combined, no two players have received more attention than have Chris Evert* (left) *and Evonne Goolagong. Although Evert lacks a major title, she was the crowd-drawer at Forest Hills in 1971. Goolagong, at 19, beat Court and King to win the Wimbledon Championship.*

peared on the cover of the *New York Times Sunday Magazine* and *Newsweek*. Suddenly bigger than Tilden, Gonzalez and Laver, her name carried far beyond sports. She fascinated housewives, doctors and bankers who had no interest in tennis. She was a budding rose in a world of thorny professionals. Everyone wanted her to win, and she did. At the $100,000 Virginia Slims finale in Florida at the end of the 1972 season, she captured the richest purse in women's tennis. But Chris was still an amateur and had to return the cash, for which the world loved her even more.

Off court, the similarity between Evert and Goolagong is striking. Both are feminine and shy. On court, they contrast definitively. Evert is precise and studied, her two-fisted backhand both an attack and a counterpunch. She has an unsophisticated serve and wages her fight from the backcourt. Goolagong makes it up as she goes along. A brilliant server, she can swoop to the net and execute the killing volley or remain in the backcourt, with her elflike footwork, and trade endless baseline exchanges. The long rally, however, is not her forte. She becomes impatient in backcourt and soon roams restlessly toward the net, seeking to interrupt her rival's pattern.

With Goolagong and Evert likely to be lifelong competitors, their rivalry may soon be distorted and sensationalized into a bitter affair. Such nonsense ought not disguise the lasting contribution to tennis that both have already made.

# Billie
# Jean
# King

94

*Sports Illustrated's Sportsman of the Year, tennis's*
*Player of the Year, Billie Jean King is the most*
*dominant force in woman's tennis—and rightfully so.*
*She is a fierce competitor as well as a natural*
*athlete. In 1971, she won more than $100,000 in prize money.*

Billie Jean King is the queen. Her playing credentials alone qualify her as the world's top player in 1972, but more important to her, Billie Jean has been the leading advocate for women's professional tennis. Almost singlehandedly, her evangelical efforts have increased prize money offered the women to half a million dollars annually. While lesser lights on the women's tour shared newly found riches, she became, in 1971, the first woman in sport to win more than $100,000 in a single year. Her efforts produced more than prizes comparable to the men's. She gained improved conditions for the women, including prime afternoon playing times rather than noon, a siesta period at most tournaments.

Developed on the rigid Southern California cement courts, her playing style is as boisterous as her off-court lobbying. She serves like a man, striving to sock the first ball deep following with a rush to net and a spiking volley. There has never been a more natural athlete playing the game. Her leaping and dashing across the court will convince any skeptic that tennis is as physically demanding as football and baseball. Mrs. King is quick to point out that in tennis unlike football, "you don't get a rest between plays. There are no half times and no time-outs. It's nonstop action for an hour and a half." And Billie Jean insists that men's

tennis is boring compared to the women's, "where the rallies are longer and serve does not dominate. You get a chance to see strategy develop." Billie Jean has collected four Wimbledon titles, one Australian and three U.S. crowns. Her eight Wimbledon doubles championships in a decade of the most severe serves and volleys ever entitles her to the sobriquet of the finest women's doubles player in the game's history. Many of her predecessors possessed potent serves or volleys or moved quickly about court, but none combined these talents as gracefully as she has. She is the consummate professional. Faced with continuous personal rivalries against Nancy Richey Gunter, Margaret Court and now the sport's Cinderella, Chris Evert, she has lost many confrontations but never avoided a challenge. She has sustained two critical knee operations that would have destroyed the mobility of a lesser competitor.

Billie Jean's proudest accomplishment was not achieved on the playing field alone. No doubt partly because of her inclination to speak her mind, *Sports Illustrated* awarded her the "Sportsman of the Year" award in 1972. Though she shared the award with UCLA basketball coach John Wooden, she was the first woman to win it. Her acceptance speech was typically to the point. "I'm very pleased. Someday a woman will stand here alone."

# The Shotmakers

4/

Since the turn of the century, the stroking styles of tennis have changed radically. Today, sleek uniforms, laminated woods and exotic metal racquets—not to mention a vastly different outlook on the game—permit shots that are far different from those prevalent in 1900, when tennis was leisurely and social and players patted the ball politely over the net. The serve, for example, once used merely as a means to put the ball in play, has become a critically important weapon. Years ago, rallies were conducted from the baseline, and the ball sometimes crossed the net more than 200 times before the point was decided. Now, every player follows his serve to the net, a maneuver that requires lightning reflexes, precision, speed and endurance. The long rally is rare; points are decided quickly and violently.

Net rushing and modern stroking style were not completely unknown to the old-timers, however. In fact, the first Wimbledon champion, Spencer Gore, was so aggressive that he often played the ball before it had crossed the net, a tactic that was soon disallowed.

But it was not until 1937 and Don Budge that a player fully explored and exploited the potential of any one shot. In reviewing accounts of the play of the masters of the early days, one soon notes that they dominated their eras because of all-around ability or a talent to capitalize on innovative technique, rather than because they possessed the ability to hit a sure winner with a single outstanding stroke.

Maurice McLaughlin, known as "the Comet," did much to move tennis from its tea-party decorum toward the hustling, crackling atmosphere of modern tennis. McLaughlin won U.S. titles in 1912 and 1913 with clever and innovative, but hardly immortal, serves and volleys. His strokes were unsophisticated forerunners of today's blockbusters.

For most of the strokes, the basic style of execution has changed little in the past 50 years.

The overwhelming changes have come in the tactics and psychology of the game. Years ago, the strategy was to keep the ball in play at all costs; the game was essentially defensive. Today, offense is the key to victory. The strategy is to end the rally as soon as possible, for players to pull all the stops and to hit away, knowing when they do so, that will decide the point one way or the other. Recently, balls have been clocked at speeds well in excess of 100 miles per hour, a velocity that our tennis ancestors probably would have termed "improper," rather than impressive.

All this is not to discount the talents and contributions of the great players of the early days of the game. It is simply that contemporary players have the advantage not only of superior equipment but also of advanced coaching and training techniques. There is little doubt that the turn-of-the-century player would be awestruck by the power game of today.

# Forehand

The forehand is the stroke that most tennis players consider the basis of their game. It is the most familiar of the strokes, and the one that beginners find the easiest to learn. Many amateurs—and even a few pros—will run halfway across the court in order to avoid a backhand and to bring the forehand into play. The forehand can be the game's hammer, marking rallies with inelegant power and blunt efficiency. But since most players can generate more accuracy as well as more power with the forward roll of the wrist than the backward, the forehand also lends itself well to the precision placement shot and the deceptive, spinning defensive shots.

One of the chief adjuncts to control in the forehand is the use of spin. Any spin slows the ball down and is therefore used principally for accuracy, though some particularly gifted players use spin for deception as well. Two spins that are used infrequently in modern play are the slice—a short, undercut stroke used almost exclusively to prepare an approach to net—and the sidespin—a hatchetlike stroke used as an alternate to a standard passing shot, as an approach preparation or for backcourt rallies. Underspin on a forehand will cause it to rise, making it ineffective against a net rusher, yet reliable for depth and control. Topspin will cause the ball to dip sharply, making it effective against the net rusher.

Although most players try to vary their strokes somewhat, depending on surface, conditions, their opponent and the situation, it is unusual for a player to employ a wide assortment of spins. It is difficult enough to respond consistently to an opponent's best shot without having to vary the spin pattern on each stroke. One exception to the rule was the legendary Bill Tilden. Although Tilden had a ferocious flat forehand, he could also garnish his shots with sidespin, underspin or topspin. He understood both the physical and psychological effects of spin better than any other player, past or present. Tilden, however, occasionally suffered from his own versatility. With so many spins from which to choose, he often selected the wrong one in the interest of creativity rather than of practical strategy.

Today's Rosie Casals exhibits a wide variety of forehand shots. She has command of the entire range of spins using many different varieties within one rally to prevent her opponent from anticipating.

The antithesis of the spinning forehand is the flat forehand, difficult to control but fast and powerful. Ellsworth Vines had perhaps the most famous flat forehand in the game—a streak that was virtually untakeable when on target. Some observers claimed that Vines's forehand was so flat that they could read the trademark on the ball as it went over the net. Although Vines's big forehand was a proficient and spectacular point winner, it left a relatively small margin for error. If his drive cleared the net by more than a few inches, it usually cleared the baseline as well.

Bill Johnston, Tilden's Davis Cup teammate and frequent foe, had a Western forehand that, though it could not be recommended to any beginner, was nonetheless perfection. "Little Bill" smacked his forehands with a force that belied his 120-pound frame. His weird, whirling windup provided violent power and spin but required too much time and too much preparation to be truly

Above: *Youngster Bill Martin runs wide of the baseline for a forehand retrieve.* Opposite: *Cliff Richey shows faultless concentration as he stares at the exact point of contact.*

effective in today's game of rapid-fire exchanges.

Jack Kramer, who played against Ellsworth Vines as a teen-ager, copied Vines's forehand but made one important change: He toned down its speed in order to gain control. Kramer could strike a rising ball and send it to the corners with superior accuracy and consistency. He also occasionally added spin, sidespin when hitting down the line and topspin when hitting cross-court. The ultimate percentage player, Kramer would never take a chance on an ego-satisfying strong-arm stroke when a safe one would serve the same purpose. His running forehand, one of the game's most celebrated strokes, had the rare combination of safety and power.

Another all-time great who used spins to his advantage was Pancho Gonzalez. While Tilden orchestrated his spins, consciously picking and choosing, Pancho—probably the closest thing to a "natural" player the game has ever known—seemed to instinctively, almost subconsciously impart spin to his forehand. When stroking from near the baseline, Pancho displayed some degree of consistency in his forehand, but as he approached the net, he became wildly unpredictable. He might chip, punch, block or hit away. He might hit with an open stance or with his back almost turned to the net, with a huge backswing or with none at all. Although Gonzalez's forehand was not one of the truly great ones, its variety and unpredictability made it a shot to be feared.

Manuel Santana, the supreme Spanish artist, had a wondrous forehand, perhaps the most versatile stroke ever. With identical motions he could send a forehand dipping drastically over the net or concoct a tantalizing dropshot that would lurch backward toward the net after landing. What Santana's forehand lacked in power, it recovered with spin, deception and control. Unable to predict the ball's direction accurately, opponents were forced to guess, often scrambling desperately to one corner of the court only to see the ball land safely in the opposite corner. Many players took Santana's topspin forehand as their example, particularly his offensive topspin lob, a shot which he developed and perfected. The lobbed ball drifted lazily to backcourt only to bound away like a frightened rabbit upon impact.

Frail and sickly as a youth, Pancho Segura discovered a way to compensate for his lack of

Above: *Jack Kramer's running forehand, one of tennis's most illustrious
strokes.* Opposite top: *Bob Lutz's aluminium racquet and nonwhite
shirt are modern trends.* Opposite bottom: *Onny Parun fetches high forehand.*

strength by developing a forehand that became his trademark throughout the tennis world. With deceptiveness equal to Santana's best, Segura's two-handed forehand proved that there is more than one way to hit any stroke. Jack Kramer and many other top pros called it the best stroke in tennis. Segura's forehand return of service was so accurate that opponents were persuaded simply never to serve to his forehand. Segura was short, and the two-handed style limited his reach, making it more difficult to get to the ball, but he compensated with uncanny anticipation and perfect footwork. More often than not, Pancho was waiting for the ball, rather than scrambling to reach it.

Don Budge possessed what was perhaps the most technically perfect forehand in the game. Until his late teens, Budge's forehand was the weakest shot in his arsenal, a weakness exploited by his opponents. Recognizing that he needed to overcome his weakness to play championship tennis, Budge switched his grip from the Western to the Eastern and sustained countless hours of drill. The tireless practice and study produced a forehand that was so consistent as to be awe-inspiring. Every Budge forehand was a replay of the one before and a forecast of the one to come. Unlike most pros, Budge did not use any wrist on his forehand. Ignoring advice to lay back his wrist and feel the ball on his racquet, thus giving himself better control and a larger margin for error, Budge stepped confidently into his forehands with his wrist locked, executed a tight, semicircular backswing, smacked the ball solidly and ended up with his racquet over his left shoulder. The result was almost always a hard, heavy shot to the corner or a zippy cross-court with little topspin. Discipline, concentration and fantastic timing turned a weakness into a winning weapon.

Among modern players, Cliff Richey displays more discipline than any of his competitors. Many pros, in their zeal to produce power, scissor one leg over the other during their follow-through. This may add power, but it significantly reduces accuracy. Even when pressured, Richey has the discipline to resist the impulse to bring his right leg over his left. Instead, he follows through straight up, keeping his feet together.

One function of discipline is concentration. To hit a forehand or any stroke perfectly, the player must maintain a riveted focus on the ball,

*Chris Evert* (opposite), *shows the importance of the left hand for balance, and though Arthur Ashe* (top) *and Kerry Melville* (bottom) *are less studied in approach, their left hands are still an integral part of their strokes.*

ignoring everything else. Chris Evert is a young player whose studied form seems awkward to many players. Chris, however, with almost hypnotic concentration, has the ability to convert mechanical detail into absolute grace, as well as winning shots.

Another vital component of the pro's forehand is his overwhelming confidence that he can hit it well under the worst possible conditions. Wind, rain and bad bounces rarely affect Arthur Ashe, who hits his forehand with an open stance and wristy follow-through that turns the racquet face completely over. Ashe has such complete and convincing confidence in himself that he can break the standard rules of form and persuade onlookers that his method is a revolutionary shortcut to winning tennis.

Aussie John Newcombe exemplifies the modern forehand style—end the rally immediately with one brutal forehand. Newcombe's backhand merely bides time until his starboard side can get into position to unload. His is not the superspinning parabola of Santana or Laver but a combination of body, arm and last-minute wrist flick that adds slight topspin for control.

Rod Laver's forehand contrasts sharply with that of Newcombe. Laver, though he varies his shots considerably, normally hits his forehand with a great deal of topspin. One reason for this style is Laver's size. Early in his career, Laver found that his flat drives tended to go long, because of the angle from which his short stature forced him to hit. He began to practice by setting up tin cans on the baseline and firing forehand drives at them. After a good deal of experimentation, Laver discovered that he could knock off the cans with considerable consistency by using topspin, which caused the ball to dip sharply just before clearing the baseline.

It is interesting that style of stroke is often a creature of environment. For example, Newcombe's bold strikes are the product of the premium placed on speed and power by the court surfaces at the world's leading championships. Forest Hills, Wimbledon and the prominent indoor events emphasize the quick kill. If grass becomes extinct—likely except at venerable Wimbledon—the Newcombe-type forehand will give way to the precision stroke of Bobby Riggs or the zippy topspin for control of Santana or Laver.

*Rod Laver* (center) *has the most feared forehand in the modern game. It is particularly dangerous because it can strike for a winner from anywhere. Nicki Pilic* (opposite top) *and Owen Davidson* (opposite bottom) *emulate Laver.*

107

# Backhand

The backhand is the most elegant step in the tennis player's ballet. Because it feels awkward, most beginners shun the backhand, preferring to hit instead the easier, though more difficult to master, forehand. A beginner is well on his way to developing a sound game when he overcomes the initial fear of his backhand and begins to hit the ball on either side with equal confidence. The backhand, without the body to obstruct follow-through, is infinitely more graceful than the forehand, with its stubby windup and awkward follow-through. Because the backhand's long backswing requires more deliberation and precision than any other stroke, it evokes a particular dramatic response when it is executed perfectly.

As with most strokes, spin plays an important part in the backhand. The three spins most commonly used in the backhand are topspin, underspin and sidespin. Topspin causes the ball to dip sharply and take a high bounce and is therefore effective for passing shots. Underspin, or slice, causes the ball to rise slightly while in the air and to stay low on impact. Accomplished players use it for sharp angle shots where control rather than power is needed, for returning low balls when approaching net and for retrieving (or desperation) shots, since the ball will hang in the air for a split second, allowing time for recovery. Sidespin causes the ball to curve toward the opponent's forehand. The sidespin backhand is used almost exclusively when going down the line and carries with it the bonus of deception. Again as with other strokes, the backhand can be hit flat, that is with no perceptible spin. Hitting the ball with no spin causes a fairly flat trajectory and a straight-through bounce. Since a flat trajectory on most backhand drives will cause the ball to go long, the flat backhand is most often used on high bouncing balls near the net.

Tilden is recognized as having had one of the best backhands of all times, but, like most players, Tilden wasn't born with a backhand. Until his middle twenties, he relied on a backhand that was merely a chop—strictly a defensive weapon, and a weak one at that. At the age of 26, Tilden finally reached the National Singles Championships, where he faced Bill Johnston. "Little Bill's" sizzling forehand completely destroyed "Big Bill's" ineffectual

*Ken Rosewall* (center), *Jim Connors* (top right) *and Stan Smith* (below right) *each exhibit from various positions the consummate grace of the backhand.*

109

backhand, and Johnston walked off with the title. The setback forced Tilden to give some thought to his backhand. He retired to Providence, Rhode Island, where he spent the winter playing on an indoor court furnished by a friend. Tilden hit backhands, stroke after stroke, day after day, all winter. The following summer, Tilden again matched his backhand against Johnston's forehand, and this time he emerged as the U.S. singles champion. Never again until age began to slow Tilden down was Johnston, or anyone else, able to dethrone him as king of the courts.

One of the most perfect, if not most potent, backhand strokes belonged to Bobby Riggs. What Riggs lacked in power he made up with perfect footwork and uncanny accuracy. His was basically a flat stroke, but on occasion he would apply spin, either topspin or slice. Though Riggs's backhand drive was not a dramatic shot, his opponents consistently found the ball landing where they didn't want it.

Lew Hoad's backhand was unusual in that he struck it almost exactly as his forehand. He used the same huge windup, the same rising follow-through. Because of his unusually strong wrist and arm, Hoad was able to get great power with this style. That Hoad was better able than most players to get down to the ball without sacrificing grace or balance, enabled him not only to hit his backhand

with more power than his competitors but to hit it at sharper angles as well.

Tony Trabert and Dick Savitt were two powerful athletes in the early 1950s who could pound backhands with both accuracy and power. Savitt's stroke was one of very few that consistently achieved maximum speed and control with sidespin. Trabert, whose style resembled Hoad's, used a more aggressive approach, hitting the ball on the rise, a tactic that set up his sudden storm to the net. This style forced him to hit under the ball, driving it upward. He is credited with being one of the first players to consistently hit a topspin backhand.

Players, writers and fans are near unanimity in the opinion that the greatest backhand of all time belonged to Don Budge. Fully 30 years after this stroke bludgeoned hapless foes into submission, Budge and the backhand are still synonymous.

Budge's backswing, with the racquet head slightly raised, was clothesline straight. The forward swing was also straight, with a firm, last-minute wrist flick at the moment of contact to give the ball a distinct topspin. The free motion was so forceful that it gave the impression of the racquet being thrown at the ball. Though Budge was capable of chipping on his backhand return of service, he usually refused to compromise and would attack with his backhand from any position on court.

Most beginners have a tendency to "run around

Opposite: *Karen Krantzke gazes hypnotically, racquet cocked, for oncoming backhand.* Above: *Cliff Drysdale, whose two-fisted backhand is as much of a rarity among the male professionals as are his belted shorts.* Left: *Roscoe Tanner, as he surveys a backhand.*

their backhand" in order to take the ball with their forehand, the shot with which they feel more confident. When trying to pressure an opponent's serve, even some pros will run around the backhand in order to emphasize offense. Though a more natural motion, the backhand is rarely an instrument of assault in its own right. To this day, it is usually relied upon for counterattack or to maneuver for position. Not for Budge. He never ran around the backhand and could strike a backhand winner from anywhere. The modern trend to defend against a net rusher with violent topspin can be traced directly to Budge.

Years after his prime, Budge would train with Jack Kramer, Dick Savitt and Chuck McKinley. None of these men, great as they were, could win by rushing net behind a delivery to Budge's backhand. His grip, prepared by sliding the thumb along the racquet handle, remains unique. Most contemporary players spurn this technique, having decided that rapid-fire exchanges at net and in the backcourt require a common grip for all strokes. This criticism is probably valid. In theory, the only way to defend against the great Budge backhand was to rush its preparation mercilessly, preventing the mighty artillery from moving into position. In practice, no one could succeed.

Virtually no player could control a topspin backhand until Budge. Topspin was the distinguishing element of his free-swinging backhand hammer. Left with the underspin backhand, relatively useless to defend against a net position, opponents surrendered an overwhelming tactical edge to Budge. His ability to attack from a position that other players could only meekly defend emphasized the preeminence of his stroke—one that many have judged to be the outstanding shot in the history of tennis.

Though most contemporary players hit a topspin backhand, Ken Rosewall continues to resist the topspin revolution. He stands alone in preventing unanimous defection from the underspin to the topspin. Rosewall's sliced stroke is surgically narrow in its margin of safety and yet can probe deep into the corners to prevent rivals from responding offensively. With a carefully carved underspin, he possesses one of the three greatest backhands of all time. Rosewall's backswing is slightly elevated; he brings the racquet down on the ball like a scythe,

*Marty Riessen* (left), *with a fencer's lunge, and Jaime Fillol* (opposite below) *and Rosie Casals* (below) *each demonstrate use of nonracquet hand to achieve poise, balance and good racquet positioning.*

causing the ball to rise as it crosses the net and to land safely in the corner of his choice. The underspin can be particularly effective on approach shots, especially on grass and clay surfaces, because the well-hit underspin will skid low, forcing the defender to hit up to the net rusher's strength.

One of the goals that Rod Laver set for himself as a youth was to become the first left-handed player ever to possess a great backhand. A glance at his record supplies conclusive proof that he succeeded. Although one of the leading proponents of the topspin backhand—the topspin in Laver's backhand, as in his forehand, helps to offset his lack of stature—Laver can with equal facility chip, dink, hit flat or with sidespin. The essential requirement for an effective topspin is a strong wrist; after uncountable hours with a squash ball and equally uncountable swings, Laver's wrist is as strong as they come. It is as massive as a mallet, and when it violently snaps over the ball, the ball sizzles over the tape with a dip that bedevils any net-rushing opponent. Those foolish enough to try to take net behind service to Laver's backhand are almost

invariably stopped in their tracks. Often they seem in danger of losing their racquets. It is impossible to consistently hit a whipping topspin deep, but Laver's topped backhand carries past the baseline after bouncing on the service line.

Because of his exceptional coordination, Laver is able to add even more zip to his backhand by taking the ball on the rise. When he strokes the ball before it has reached the high point of its bounce, he makes use of his opponent's pace to impart more speed to the ball, to break his opponent's rhythm and to force his opponent to hurry to reach the ball.

Nicola Pilic and Owen Davidson are two players who have copied Laver's stroke and tried to master the topspin backhand. Both have tried to overcome the inherent weakness in a slice backhand by coming under the ball and imparting topspin by sharply rolling the wrist upward at the moment of contact. Laver, Pilic and Davidson, all left-handers, have the added advantage of usually playing against right-handers, who are not accustomed to playing lefties.

Opposite: *Carole Graebner, like most other woman players, slices her backhand because her wrist is not strong enough to roll over ball.*
Above: *Rod Laver, whose wrist is iron, sometimes elects to underspin.*

# Forehand Volley

The volley—hitting the ball before it bounces—provides punctuation to the rally, punctuation that is often final. A player prepares the conclusion through groundstroke exploitation of angles and depth, setting the stage for the *coup de grace* through a dramatic volley. The development of the volley has, perhaps, changed the game of tennis more than any other single stroke. No longer are players content to stay at the baseline and hit groundstroke after groundstroke, patiently waiting for their opponents to make a mistake. Servers nowadays will take net behind almost every serve, for the man who controls the net invariably controls the play. And the way to control the net and win the point once there is by volleying. Of course, a volley can be hit from anywhere on the court, but it is most effective and dramatic at net. The defensive player's job is to pass the net man or to hit a lob deeply and accurately enough to gain control of the net for himself. Just as the overhead is the answer to the defensive lob, the volley is the answer to the attempted passing shot.

Volley exchanges are so fast that even pros often find it impossible to keep their eyes on the ball. Most pros, however, have logged so many hours on the court that they develop an instinct, an intuition that enables them to get the racquet on the ball. Guesswork alone, of course, will not succeed. (Chuck McKinley saved his "crash-guess" volley for desperate situations, when the only possible way to save the point was by making a lucky guess.) In order to volley successfully in a consistent manner, the player must have a knowledge of the dynamics of the ball in flight, a knowledge of his opponent's style, lightning-fast reflexes, confidence and more than a little courage.

The volley is unlike any other tennis stroke; it is not really a stroke at all, but rather a punch. Normally hit with a locked wrist, the volley utilizes the opponent's pace—it is more of a rebound than a stroke. The forehand volley—and the backhand volley as well—is almost invariably hit with underspin, achieved by tilting the racquet face up as the forearm punches forward in a swing usually no longer than a foot. Since volleys are often hit at sharp angles, the underspin is invaluable in giving a player added control and touch. There is one situa-

Left: *John Newcombe can take full swing at forehand volley because ball rises high over the net.* Above: *Rod Laver must limit his swing to a punch action because ball has just skimmed net, dropping quickly afterward.*

*Derek Schroeder* (preceding page) *and Cliff Drysdale* (above) *illustrate that the action around the net is often so fast they don't have time to watch the ball strike the racquet. Instead they must hope to anticipate its flight.*

tion in which the volley is hit flat: when the opponent has made a mistake and the return is sitting high, soft and fat. For the put-away, control is forsaken for power.

The drop volley, or dump shot, though used relatively infrequently, is a potent adjunct to the volley. The drop volley is hit at sharper angles and with more underspin than the volley. Executed properly, the drop volley is a sure winner. Executed improperly, it is a sure loser; if the opponent manages to get to the ball, it is a simple matter for him to put it away. The drop volley is hit by opening the racquet face to a greater degree than in a normal volley and by bringing the racquet face under the ball at the moment of impact by means of a wrist flick. Because of the inherent danger of the tactic and the relatively small margin for error, most players will use the drop volley only when they can find no suitable alternative.

Because of his size and reach, his natural instincts and his great mobility, Pancho Gonzalez was exceptionally effective at net. For the same reasons, he was able to play closer to the net than most players before or since. This tight-in position, though dangerous, gave him an advantageous angle and made his volleys even more lethal. Pancho's first volleys often kicked up chalk on the baseline, and he managed to effect seemingly impossible angles on his volleys. Using the hammer grip on the forehand side, Pancho almost always hit with underspin. He was also a master of the drop volley. Like most other players, Pancho used excessive underspin to take speed off his drop volley, but his drop shot had an extra dimension. At the moment of contact, before bringing his racquet through and under the ball, Pancho moved his racquet slightly backward, a precision maneuver that requires such split-second timing and perfect coordination as to be beyond the reach of all but the extremely gifted.

Although Bill Tilden preferred to win his points from the baseline, he possessed a superb forehand volley. Though he played in an era in which the net game was not emphasized, Tilden was an extraordinary strategist and recognized the value of an occasional sortie to the net. When at net, Tilden's long reach and perfect footwork stood him in good stead. Able to cover the court in just a few swooping strides, he was seldom passed. As the leading master of spins, Tilden was, not surprisingly, the master of the drop volley. Once booed at

Wimbledon for using the drop shot, Tilden was the man responsible for making the drop shot and the drop volley part of every player's repertoire.

Bobby Riggs had an arsenal full of potent strokes, but the shot he most depended on was the volley. Never a power hitter, Riggs relied on touch, control and accuracy to make his forehand volley a consistent winner. Possibly the hardest shot in the Riggs game was his high volley on the forehand side. He hit this shot in much the same manner as he did the overhead, simply shortening both the backswing and the follow-through. Bobby could consistently put away the high ones, but most of the time, he played the angles and the percentages, punching the forehand volley from the shoulder with his wrist locked. Interestingly, the net revolution took place in the middle of Riggs's career. For years he had been a baseline player, relying on consistency in his groundstrokes to outlast the competition. But the times and style of play changed, and so did Riggs. Though hampered by lack of height and reach, Riggs learned to come to the net. Not only was Riggs versatile enough to change his style, he was also talented and determined enough to become one of the best volleyers of all time.

John Bromwich, the great Australian player, probably hit the ball softer than any player ever to compete in topflight tennis. He was known, on occasion, to hit 25 drives, each landing within inches of the last, just to win a single point. Power players the world over blasted away at him, but somehow the ball always came back. One of his coaches once likened him to a practice wall. Bromwich's game was not awesome, just consistent—until he got to net. At the net, Bromwich displayed speed, agility and flexibility that was almost supernatural. He might handle a searing drive with a left-handed forehand volley, follow it up with a two-handed volley on the right side, then terminate the point with a right-handed smash. The unorthodox Bromwich (who was talked into giving up his two-handed service when in his early teens) could execute these shots in an instant while zipping from one end of the net to the other, displaying speed, control and versatility that demoralized opponents.

The outstanding aspect of Lew Hoad's net game was his ability to get down to the ball. Since the volley is hit with the racquet higher than the wrist, Hoad's ability to get right down to the ground without bending his back was invaluable to him in digging out low balls near the net. On the low, defensive volleys, which he hit with a locked wrist, Hoad seldom missed. On higher balls, however, Hoad elected to go with a full stroke, rather than the abbreviated punch stroke that most players prefer. Though the style gained him power, he sacrificed accuracy, and his waist-high volley was inconsistent, often sailing wide or catching the net.

Pancho Segura, Frank Sedgman and John Newcombe are probably the premier forehand volleyers of this or any other era, yet their styles have almost nothing in common. Segura could vary his two-handed scimitar to smoke volleys in any direction or delicately drop volley a foe to frustration. Pancho's forehand volley, like his forehand drive, had an enviable accuracy and consistency. His speed and grace at net and his unrivaled tactical savvy made him next to impossible to pass. Because he was short, he did not have to go into a deep crouch to sight balls that barely cleared the tape. This fact, coupled with his amazing agility, made him incomparable at digging out the low ball and blocking the down-the-line blast. One of Segura's techniques set a perfect example for the weekend player: He never worried about the net as an obstacle. He merely chose his target and hit away on the forehand volley, completely ignoring the net. This psychological tactic greatly increased the one ingredient necessary to be successful—confidence.

Frank Sedgman, "the Aussie Lamb," relied almost exclusively on a marvelous hand-eye coordination and a quickness that enabled him to make forehand put-aways as though the ball had come to him in slow motion. He gave spectators the impression that he was playing on top of the net, though in fact he maintained a safe margin between himself and the barrier. It was simply that he had such exceptional lateral swiftness that he could cut off passing shots a fraction of a second after they had cleared the net. Sedgman was one of a few players who have been able to combine power with accuracy, and the percentage of his volleys that were unreturnable was amazingly high.

Newcombe's forehand strength has set the pattern for all contemporary volleyers. He is not as fleet as Sedgman, nor are his reflexes the equal of Segura's, but he prepares his passage to the net with such certainty that the rally is his for the killing. Behind his powerful serve, Newcombe is probably the most effective volleyer in the game today.

122

*Australian Ian Fletcher is able to focus on the moment of contact even after the ball has struck and left his racquet.*

# Backhand Volley

Volleyers may be proficient at several techniques, but few are decisive at all levels of this difficult stroke. In most cases, the reason for this difficulty is simple: lack of practice. During actual play, the volley is simply not hit that often. The ratio of groundstrokes compared to volleys—even in practice—is at least 10 to 1 in favor of groundstrokes. The truly great volleyers refine their art by practicing under pressure, spending hour after hour in drills, stretching and diving for hard shots. Few waste time during drills by simply dumping the ball straight back to their sparring partner.

Though the forehand volley and the backhand volley are comparably difficult to execute, most players express a preference for the backhand. One reason for this is the fact that the motion away from the body is freer. Another is that shots that are hit close to the body are more manageable on the backhand side than on the forehand.

The backhand volley is, not surprisingly, quite similar to the forehand volley. It is also more of a punch than a stroke and is almost invariably hit with underspin. Most players use the same grip that they use on the backhand drive, use an abbreviated backswing and follow-through and hit with a firm wrist. On high volleys the backhand, just as the forehand, is sometimes hit flat, but to achieve a great deal of power on this stroke requires a stronger than average wrist.

Although most players prefer to drop volley from the forehand side, many can effect this shot with equal or even superior results from the backhand. As in the forehand, the drop volley is achieved by opening the racquet face to a greater degree than in the regular volley and by punching under the ball.

The half volley—taking the ball immediately after the bounce—once had little purpose other than appealing to the grandstand. Nowadays, this shot is an important part of every player's repertoire. It can be hit from either side with equal efficiency and is an invaluable aid when one is caught in "no-man's land" en route to net. The half volley is usually hit in much the same way as the volley, though some players—usually those with exceptional timing and hand-eye coordination—can get away with stroking it. Stroking the half volley will add speed and weight to the ball, but the small margin for error involved in this maneuver makes it risky for the great majority of players.

Although novice players are advised to play their net game about halfway between the net and the service line, a few professionals—Jack Kramer was one—have been able to force their opponent's game by playing closer to the net. Kramer was the first pro to consistently rush net behind every service. Once Kramer had reached the net, the point was soon ended, one way or the other. Though Kramer was not one of the all-time great volleyers, his approach was so strong that it made his net game one of the strongest ever. His volleys were deep, and he patrolled the net so well that opponents had difficulty passing him. Kramer's backhand volley did not have the power of his forehand, but what it lacked in speed it recovered in accuracy. Whether the ball was high or low, Kramer hit the same way—with good underspin and unerring aim.

Unlike Kramer, Don Budge almost never took net behind service. Budge played a deliberate game, staying back and carving out points with his solid groundstrokes. Occasionally, however, after preparing the way carefully, he would take net. Once there, he preferred to stroke anything that came at him at waist-level or higher. He could use touch when he wanted to, digging up low balls and delicately returning them in sharp-angled drop volleys, but Budge placed his real faith in power. If his backhand drive was potent, his backhand volley was devastating. Shortening

*Mike Estep's form exemplifies perfectly the axiom "bend the knees for the volley," as his crouch dips most of his body below the net. From this defensive position, only a safe, steady volley can result.*

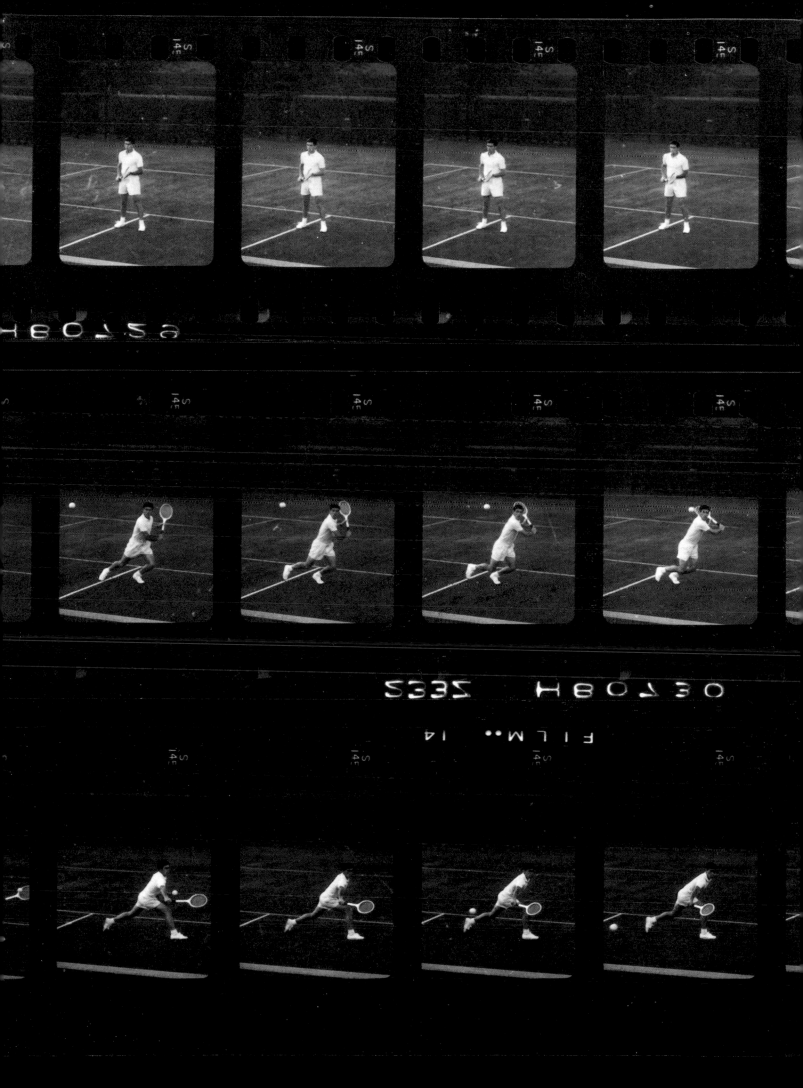

his backswing only a trifle, Budge would blast away at an attempted passing shot. The result was a flat, vicious blast that opponents could seldom reach, let alone return. Because of his magnificent timing, Budge attained a consistency on his stroked backhand volley that most punch-volleyers would envy.

Another player who preferred to stroke on the backhand volley was Bobby Riggs. On the forehand side, Riggs consistently used the punch, but when hitting the backhand volley he used a miniature version of his backhand drive. Riggs, like Budge, had a picture-perfect backhand drive, the explanation, perhaps, of his preference for the stroke volley on the backhand. Also like Budge, Riggs achieved an impressive consistency with his backhand volley.

Although Lew Hoad's forehand volley has occasionally been criticized, no one has ever found fault with his volley off the backhand. A large reason for the potency of Hoad's net game was his blazing speed in getting to net. Hoad was also one of the few players who has been able to gamble, playing right at the net and getting away with it. The overwhelming majority of his backhand volleys ended the point immediately. Scrupulous in his preparation for hitting the backhand volley, Hoad drove it with consistently winning form. The shot was punched with wrist locked. He hit the ball with more underspin—and occasional sidespin—than most other players.

One of the many reasons for Dennis Ralston's consistent success at net is his uncanny eyesight. Ralston is one of the few players in the history of tennis who is able to take almost every ball on the rise. This not only enables him to make use of his opponent's pace, it also greatly facilitates and strengthens his rush to net. Ralston finds taking the ball on the rise particularly helpful because he is not known for one of the bigger first serves in the game. The other reason for Ralston's success at the net is that he possesses a great volley from either side. His 6-foot 2-inch frame gives him an exceptional reach, and he has the mobility to extend that reach from sideline to sideline. The same phenomenal eyesight and hand-eye coordination that enables Ralston to get to net allows him to pound away once there. His quickness of eye gets him to the ball early enough to take a short backswing, but that backswing is one that is long enough to give him all the additional

Preceding pages: *Ken Rosewall releases a full swing on a backhand volley.* Right: *Jeanne Evert suffers like a weekender when hurried.*

leverage necessary to really powder the tennis ball.

Rod Laver, Tony Roche and Ken Rosewall are generally acknowledged as the most formidable backhand volleyers in tennis today. Laver backs up his prowess at net with equally formidable prowess on the overhead. If an opponent attempts to lob over Laver, his reward is a smoking smash that usually bounds from the court to the grandstand. If an opponent attempts to hit through or pass Laver, the result is a lethal volley that is almost always out of racquet's reach. With his great mobility and potent volleys, Laver has convinced more than one opponent that the net is an impenetrable barrier when he is standing sentry. The outstanding reason that Laver's backhand volley is such a fearsome weapon is his massive, powerful left wrist. Though most players have difficulty generating power on the backhand volley, the mighty roll of Laver's wrist sends the ball streaking with incredible speed. The power of his wrist also enables him to hit the volley at angles ordinary players find impossibly sharp. Laver is competent and consistent on the low, defensive volley, and he is short enough to experience little difficulty in getting down to the ball. On shots waist-level or higher, however, he is murderous. Early in his career, Laver consistently creamed volleys at this height, but lately he has taken to conserving energy by playing the angles and hitting the ball only hard enough to ensure putting it away.

From left to right: *Andres Gimeno frets over the backhand overhead; John Newcombe parries with a fencer's lunge; Rod Laver shows his supreme confidence at net; Frenchman N'Godrilla struggles to make contact.*

When called for, however, the power is still there. Laver too has the ability to take the ball on the rise, an attribute that not only enhances his charge to the net, but also makes him deadly on the half volley.

Tony Roche's backhand volley is, perhaps, even heavier than Laver's, because he is inclined to take a longer backswing and to follow through to a greater degree. Though slightly less consistent than Laver, Roche, with the eye of a sharpshooter, can turn around a match with this stroke.

Ken Rosewall has the unusual ability to take a healthy cut with his backhand volley at anything that clears the net by more than a foot. Rosewall's backswing is not elongated behind his body but is elevated behind his head so that he can stroke down on the ball decisively. For the sake of precision, Rosewall seldom hits flat but sharply slices the ball so that his opponent will have to dig the low ball out and hit upward, thus setting up the put-away. Having one of the strongest and most consistent backhand drives in the history of the game, Rosewall can hit away in backhand volley situations where most players would be content to merely punch. At net, Ken is never tentative in his thrusts, refusing to accept the defensive block as an alternative. Coupling his excellent volleying ability with extreme quickness and confidence, Rosewall is able to cover the net, seldom leaving an opening that an opponent can exploit.

# Serve

The evolution of the serve has paralleled the game's erratic and volatile history. From the sport's beginnings, in the courtyards of French monasteries 700 years ago, the serve was simply a ceremonial gesture to place the ball in play. That master innovator, Major Walter Clopton Wingfield, continued the custom with his "sphairistike," which was more or less the modern father of lawn tennis.

Today, the serve is the single most important factor in tennis. The accuracy and weight of the serve cannot vary with the ability or tactics of the foe. As a result, the serve is executed with a ferocity that is seldom seen during a rally, where concessions must be made to the opponent's game. Points and games are now won outright with the player's delivery of a crushing serve, often without need for a follow-up volley or approach shot. For today's players, the big serve is standard. In short, aces abound.

Modern, fast surfaces have diminished the length of rallies to such an extent that many modern innovators have begun to devise schemes to reduce the lethal effectiveness of the serve. Some of the more practical suggestions that have been offered are serving three feet behind the baseline, prohibiting the server from advancing to net until after the receiver has hit his return and eliminating service faults, thereby limiting the number of serves to one per point. There have also been more obvious, if somewhat harsher suggestions, such as the one offered by Hall of Famer Bill Talbert: "Have the players work on their service returns." The most likely changes, however, are the slowing down of playing surfaces and the reducing of the speed components of the ball. Whatever the changes, one hopes they will not alter the inherent excitement of the service ace, the equivalent of baseball's home run and football's "bomb."

The serve is the most personal stroke in tennis. It identifies the player as definitely as a number on a jersey identifies a football player. A player's service, mainly because it is not dependent on the opposition for placement, rarely changes. The style is developed early in the pro's career, and once cast, remains constant.

When novices ask about the proper grip and follow-through for the serve, the wisest answer is

*Bob McKinley, though just a rookie pro,*
*can strike with the same vengeance on serve as can*
*the most experienced superstar.*

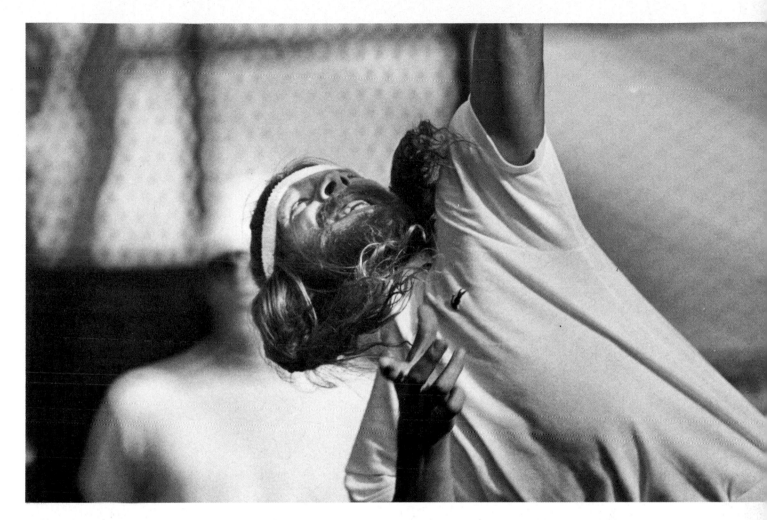

that there is no one way to play any shot. This advice holds true in many sports, but in no other sport is individual application as admissible as in tennis—especially in the serve. Despite the enormous variety of service styles, some common denominators of good form are accepted, and a few players have service motions that are technically so sound that they are borrowed as models for line drawings in instruction booklets. The stretch of the arm to its maximum height at the moment of impact is universal. The age-old maxim, "Keep your eye on the ball," while important everywhere, is especially critical during the serve. Most players agree that the smooth, continuous motion, devoid of hitches and pauses, will consistently produce the best serve. The ideal serve is the one that can deliver the ball flat, with slice or with twist from the identical motion, thus disguising from the opponent the spin on the ball until after it strikes.

The flat service is achieved by snapping the wrist and opening the racquet face on impact. One follows through to the opposite side of the racquet hand. The flat serve is the powerhouse serve, and is usually aimed for a corner or for the opponent's weakness. The slice serve is achieved by hitting around the ball in a motion similar to that used in the chip shot. The follow-through for the slice serve is the same as that for the flat serve. The slice serve is effective for drawing the opponent out of court and is especially useful against an opponent with a weak forehand. On fast surfaces, such as grass, it will skid rather than bounce, forcing the receiver to hit up to the net rusher. The American twist service is hit by tossing the ball slightly farther behind the head than usual and hitting up and over the ball. One follows through slightly higher than in the other two services and in the direction of the racquet hand; that is, to the right for right-handers, to the left for left-handers. The motion used in hitting the American twist imparts a great deal of topspin to the ball. The twist, therefore, is used almost exclusively for second serves, since the dipping

*Wendy Overton's left hand holds onto the second ball after the first is released (opposite). Most young pros stuff the reserve ball into a pocket, a problem for women and Torben Ulrich who doesn't understand pockets (above).*

characteristic of topspin makes it possible to clear the net by a comfortable margin while running minimum risk of hitting long.

John Doeg and Ellsworth Vines characterized, though in different ways, the early power deliveries. Doeg was a left-hander whose vicious left-to-right slice was almost solely responsible for his winning the United States Championships in 1930. Vines succeeded Doeg as national champion in 1931 and won again in 1932 with a fistful of fierce, flat strokes. The most telling of them was a smoking, spinless serve, which, when on the mark, was literally untakeable.

Jack Kramer was the first exponent of the big game. His groundstrokes and volleys alone were not

overwhelming, and his service speed has since been exceeded by a dozen or more players, but he put all the elements together to play the percentages. He went to net on every serve, not just occasionally. His first serve was slightly sliced and always deep and well-placed. His second serve was a perfect copy of the first, but he rarely had to hit a second serve. Kramer had perfect control over the urge to shoot for an ace when in trouble. He played the percentages, taking a little speed off the first ball so that there wouldn't have to be a second and consistently hitting the ball to his opponent's weakness. True, Kramer served proportionately few aces, but his serve was strong enough to maintain the offensive, and when the receiver returned the serve to

Opposite: *Charlie Pasarell has one
of the most envied service motions
in tennis.* Below: *Chris Evert
has worked on her one weak serve
to give it force and reliability,
but her motion is still uneasy and cramped.*

Above: *Ilie Nastase's serve, while solid, does not distinguish him from other pros.* Right: *Ian Fletcher is a young professional who knows the need of a big serve. He trains on this stroke more than any other.*

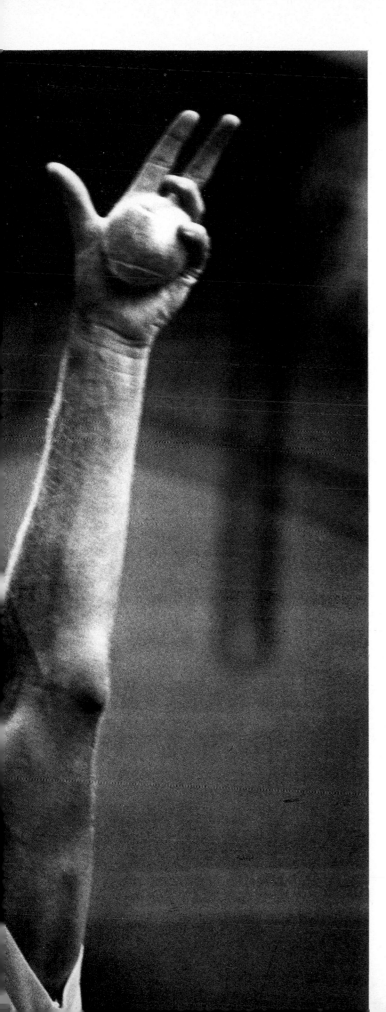

him, Kramer was invariably at the net, waiting for it.

The most formidable serve in the history of the game belonged exclusively to Pancho Gonzalez. The Gonzalez serve, along with the Budge backhand, is the most talked about and respected stroke in tennis. At 6 feet 3 inches, Gonzalez had the necessary height to get the proper angle for his blazing, flat first service. At one time or another, most of the great names in tennis have watched the Gonzalez first serve whistle by unmolested. Gonzalez himself has admitted that during his early years it was his big serve that kept him at or near the top, staving off competitors while his other strokes developed. Crisis seemed to sharpen Pancho's eye—the number of aces he served on "must have" points is incredible. Although Gonzalez had the ability to hit serves effectively and deceptively with any spin he chose, he usually reserved his spinning shots for the second serve. Whether hitting the flat sizzler or the deceptive spinner, Gonzalez's motion was the same, never flamboyant, neither big nor small, but simply fluid, graceful and as precise as clockwork. There is an aphorism in tennis that once you have learned a fluid service motion, you never forget its essentials, no matter how inactive or old you become. Pancho epitomizes this rule. He is inactive at present, having retired and unretired more than any other athlete, and now he is old (44) by tennis standards. Yet his service action today is still flawless, an awesome combination of grace and power. His frame, tall and lean, is perfect for the serve, and he never lacks the confidence to strike an ace, regardless of the score. His ability to hurl unplayable bolts in crisis situations gave rise to Pancho's famous credo, "When I'm down love–40 on my serve, it's like I'm even."

Lew Hoad's right-to-left slice served as a model for his fellow pros and was particularly effective in serving wide to the forehand in the deuce court. Hoad could also unload with the flat ace, as well as cross up the receiver with the unpredictable bounce of an American twist. Hoad's wrist, as strong as a bear trap, snapped at the last moment, leaving his opponent no chance to anticipate the direction of the serve. An unusual aspect of Hoad's serve was a jumping foot flutter at the moment of delivery.

While winning the championship at Wimbledon in 1963, Chuck McKinley demonstrated that he was one of the world's leading practitioners of the American twist. In marching to the championship without losing a set, McKinley proved he was one of the games smartest servers. Relying on various speeds of the twist and mixing in an occasional flat shot, McKinley, a short 5 feet 8 inches, prevented his opponents from concentrating on any one particular delivery. He breezed through the final in three straight sets, winning every one of his service games.

Stan Smith, at 6 feet 4 inches, has the height to make him one of the best servers of all time. Opponents have been heard to remark that receiving service against him is like letting someone fire at you from a treetop. In winning the U.S. Open final in 1971, Smith rapped in a total of 66 out of 97 first serves. Serving at 5–6 in the fourth set of that final against Jan Kodes, Smith proved not only that he could come through in a tight situation, but also that he kept more than one service in his locker. He won the last three points of the game from the baseline. The first was an untakeable flat powerhouse. The last two were spinning, wildly bouncing aces.

The only player today who consistently recognizes that a vital element of service is the subsequent motion to the net is John Newcombe. Newcombe is the complete server. He consistently scores with his hard, first-serve slice and finishes his follow-through at the beginning of his burst to the net. Newcombe's first volley is usually hit from a foot inside the service line, a method that greatly improves the volley. Other players have gotten to the net faster but behind vastly weaker serves. Other players have been able to hit a stronger serve but have not been able to move to the net as quickly. Newcombe combines a solid serve with the move to net better than any other man in the game's history.

As services become faster, the need becomes obvious for electronic devices to replace the human linesmen. In the backgrounds of each of the surrounding pictures is a linesman waiting to cast judgment as to whether a ball is in or out. Gonzalez, Newcombe and John Alexander, a young pretender to Newcombe's serving throne, all serve at speeds in excess of 125 miles per hour. Needless to say, at these speeds it is difficult for a man positioned more than 10 yards away to make accurate calls in situations that may involve fractions of an inch.

*Patrico Dominquez* (top left), *Torben Ulrich* (top right), *Cliff Richey* (near right), *Dominquez again* (center right) and *Tom Gorman* (far right), *all show through contortions of mouth and eyes the strain of the serve. The serve is their opening move and, perhaps, their last move as well.*

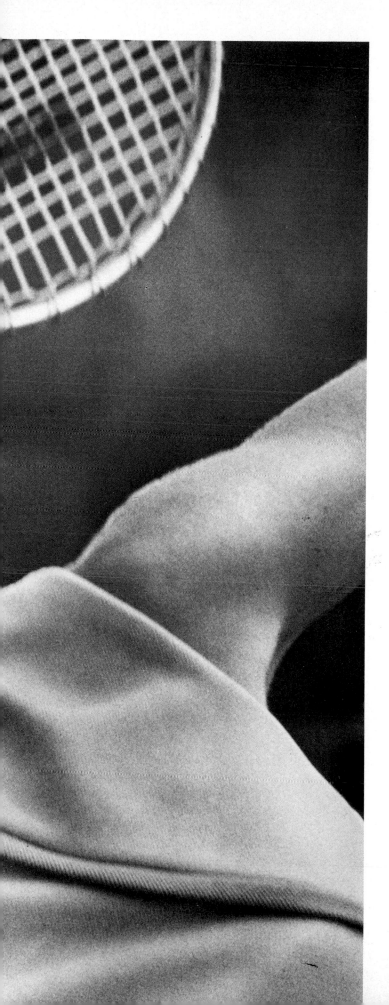

# Overhead

It is often said that the overhead is the same as the serve, and in many ways this comparison is accurate. Certainly, as a training aid the visual comparison is invaluable. In actuality, however, there is a great difference between the two strokes. The serve can be hit at the server's leisure. He can take time to decide what he wants to do with a particular serve and to concentrate on his form. He can adjust his toss on windy days or even let the ball drop to the ground if he is not satisfied with it. He can adjust his stance if the sun is in his eyes. The overhead, on the other hand, is not so flexible. The player must hit the overhead when and where he finds it, regardless of wind, sun or court conditions. In a few seconds, the player must backpedal from the net, get into position, execute the backswing, evaluate his opponent's position, make a tactical decision as to where and at what speed he wants the ball to go and then hit the ball. The backswing on the overhead is, of necessity, usually shorter than that of the serve, though the follow-through is similar. Also, while the serve can be hit with a variety of spins, most players prefer to hit the overhead flat. Some good players will occasionally garnish it with slice. Ironically, many players who have a weak serve have exceptionally strong overheads. One explanation for this phenomenon is that the enlarging of the target area to an entire court relieves psychological tensions and allows the player to hit away without fear of sending the ball out of bounds.

The overhead is the antithesis of the defensive lob and, as such, is vital to the net game. No matter how well a player may volley, he must possess a consistent, potent overhead if he expects to win points at the net, points which are critically important to successfully contest the match. The player who runs around a defensive lob and responds with a defensive lob of his own will more often than not find himself on the losing side.

One of the best overheads of all time belonged, not surprisingly in view of his prowess as a server, to Pancho Gonzalez. Pancho could smash the ball and put it away for good, but he was equally proficient at the precision placement shot.

Chuck McKinley's overhead was the most dramatic and most effective overhead in the history of

*Julie Heldman's racquet drops down to "backscratching"*
*position, which is as essential to the overhead as it is to the serve.*
*In hitting both strokes, her eyes never leave the ball.*

tennis. The sight of McKinley leaping high to bury a smash will remain vivid for all who ever saw him. McKinley was a smart server, varying spins for deception and change of pace, but because of his shortness he could never consistently hit the hard, fast serve. When he got a shot at an overhead, he would pound it savagely, as if to avenge his limitation in serving.

Early in his career, McKinley recognized that because of his lack of reach at the net it was necessary for him to develop an exceptional overhead in order to be effective at net. The obvious way to improve any stroke is through practice and coaching. McKinley devoted countless hours to both. He hit overhead after overhead and diligently studied the techniques of other players. He learned the angles. He learned when to smash and when to go for placement. He learned when to take the ball in the air and when to let the ball bounce before putting it away. In the end, his tireless efforts gave him the best overhead smash of all time.

Bobby Riggs and Ken Rosewall both relied on uncanny accuracy and faultless strategy in their overheads. Bill Talbert was full of guile in using angles to put away smashes. McKinley's style was brute strength. He was a master at bouncing the ball out of the stadium. If a foe was within reach of the ball, the ball either blew past him or bowled him over. Although Chuck never purposely aimed his overhead smash at an opponent, he felt that he had the right to aim his smash at any portion of the court, without regard to his opponent's position. If the ball and the opponent happened to arrive at the same spot at the same time . . . well, it was regrettable, but it was a point. McKinley used a heavy racquet and had an exceptionally strong forearm. No other player ever hit an overhead as hard.

The poach, that deceptive doubles shuffle used to intercept a ball at net, is the tactical ally of the overhead. It is not surprising that the same man should be the best at both enterprises. Again, McKinley's style was destruction rather than guile. A McKinley poach could physically punish an opponent, whether it struck racquet or player, a fact that tended to unsettle opponents and make McKinley's poaches even more effective.

McKinley possessed all the equipment necessary to hit a good overhead or poach. His feet were quick, he could jump well and his hands were keyed to his eyes as if there were an eye in every

fingertip. These qualities combined to make it virtually impossible to defend against McKinley at net.

McKinley was also the innovator of the "crash-guess" interception, a sort of poach against a poach. When a defender moved across to pick off a service return, McKinley, also at net, would guess at the direction of the volley and swing mightily at the same time. If he connected, his opponent's life was at stake. If not, the vicious swipe was so intimidating that his foe usually didn't care to venture to poach for the remainder of the match.

Preceding pages: *John Newcombe's overhead is as devastating as his serve.* Above: *Lesley Hunt's athleticism is as respected as the versatility* (opposite) *of Rosie Casals.*

# Mobility and Speed

Although mobility and speed, like athleticism and competitiveness, are not tennis strokes, any professional regards these qualities as the heart of a player's ability. Most players would gladly trade a solid backhand or forehand for quickness and mobility. No matter how good a player's strokes, they are worthless if he can't reach the ball in time to hit it.

Speed in a tennis match is not reckoned in quite the same manner as speed at a track meet. The man who can sprint 100 yards in fewer than 10 seconds cannot automatically translate his speed into tennis terms. Speed in tennis is a strange mixture of intuition, guesswork, footwork and hair-trigger reflexes. Many of the players famed for quickness on the court would finish dead last in a field of schoolgirls in a race of any distance more than 10 yards.

Bill Tilden, still the choice of many as the greatest all-around tennis player of all time, would probably have been appalled at the idea of anything as barbaric as a footrace. But on the tennis court, Tilden's 6-foot 3-inch, 165-pound frame moved with deceptive quickness. His long, swooping strides and his impeccable footwork enabled him to traverse the court seemingly without exertion in split seconds. Off court Tilden smoked cigarettes almost continuously, but the habit never seemed to affect his on-court performance. Always in peak condition, Tilden's ability to get to the ball and to deal with it when he got there made him even more outstanding on defense than he was on offense.

Five-foot four-inch Bitsy "the Atlanta Atom" Grant's short legs would never have carried him to any first place medals in a high-school track meet, yet he was one of the best retrievers in the history of tennis. Known as a defensive specialist, Grant could reach and return almost any shot. It was simply a matter of time until his opponent made a mistake, and they recurred more and more frequently as a match wore on. Strangely enough, even though Bitsy was the one doing the running, his opponent was the one to tire. Part of Grant's ability lay in anticipation, but a good deal of it had to do with courage. As far as Bitsy was concerned, no ball was out of his reach.

Pancho Gonzalez best exemplifies that the big man can be as fleet as the small man. Most players

*Three ingredients are necessary for outstanding mobility: anticipation, acceleration and simple quickness afoot. Tom Okker's 130-pound frame facilitates overall speed.*

go into a crouch immediately before hitting the ball and straighten up immediately after hitting, a movement that costs precious tenths of seconds. Pancho folds his 6-foot 3-inch frame up into a leopardlike crouch at the beginning of a match and never straightens up until the last point is finished. The same intuition that permits Pancho to almost instinctively hit the right shot with the right spin to the right place also helps him in his court movement. Gonzalez is moving "at the crack of the bat," sometimes before, and whether his opponent attempts to pass him down the line, lob over him or angle past him with a sharp overhead, Pancho's uncanny ball sense, the knack of being in the right place at the right time, enables him to reach the ball with ease.

Rod Laver didn't pick up the nickname "the Rocket" by accident. It had a lot to do with the way in which he moved on a tennis court. As with some other players, Laver's ability to cover a court is not based on pure physical speed alone. A combination of instinct, savvy and grim determination

lets the redhead reach the seemingly unreachable ball. Laver combines a fierce net game with the quickness necessary to get back for the overhead. And when a lob is too deep for the overhead, Laver has the speed and wrist strength to run around it, take it on the bounce and crack back a winner.

Rafe Osuna and Alex Almedo both were fast as sprinters. They could use their speed in charging the net behind service and in runing down balls that would have been out of reach to players of average speed. They were able to overcome their lack of power games by getting second and third chances on shots that would have been unplayable for most pros.

Tom Okker, with a small, strong frame, has the ideal build for mobility. Most bigger men have difficulty in switching their movement from right to left or switching from forehand to backhand. Okker's lightness and compactness enhance his natural speed and quickness. His extraordinary body control can trick the spectator's eyes, as sometimes he seems to change direction in midair.

Opposite: *Alex Almedo has the natural speed of a sprinter.*
Above: *Evonne Goolagong never makes spectators conscious of her speed—her fluid gait gives the impression that she floats above the court.*

# Competitiveness

Competitiveness combines many elusive elements, some of which are distinct frames of mind: the understanding that the 30–15 point is more important than the 40–0 point; the understanding that no matter how far ahead you may be in a match, you can't afford to let up; the understanding that no matter how far behind you may be in a match, it's still possible to pull it out; and the understanding that even when a situation is hopeless, when defeat is imminent, you must fight down to the last point.

Every top tennis professional is a top competitor. Some are more skilled, more physically gifted than others. Some are smaller, a bit less quick, a bit less strong than others and yet seem to have some indefinable quality, some unknown element that enables them to emerge as winners. These are the truly great competitors—those who are forced to rely on combativeness, on the will to win, to overcome a lack of natural physical gifts.

Bitsy Grant, for example, "the Atlanta Atom," was 5 feet 4 inches and weighed 120 pounds, yet he scratched out victories in countless matches that by objective reckoning he should have lost. He beat Ellsworth Vines at Forest Hills, 6–3, 6–3, 6–3, in 1933, when Vines was ranked first in the world. He thrashed Don Budge on clay at White Sulphur Springs in a match that Southerners refused to call an upset.

Bobby Riggs was another player who was short and small, but whose stature was gigantic as a competitor. Unlike other small players, who relied on defending and retrieving, Riggs had enormous racquet virtuosity and could attack or defend equally well. Riggs added the dimension of gamesmanship to competitiveness. No one could outthink or "outpsych" him, and he was always toughest when the money was up and the chips were down.

Pancho Segura also gave away height and weight to almost every opponent he faced, but as possessor of the best tennis mind ever he more than made up for the deficit. Segura always gave his best and would never think of letting up even in the most insignificant mixed doubles match. He ran down wayward balls relentlessly, and every fiber of his small body lent impetus to his two-handed smashes, which bigger men found next to impos-

*Jeanne Evert, 15, has nothing to lose when competing against older, more experienced, professionals. Since she is not yet expected to win, pressure is removed.*

sible to handle. The breadth of his competitive and intuitive talents is made clear by the fact that every top pro fortunate enough to know him came to him for guidance in tactics and strategy. Segura was even known to counsel both players who were facing each other in a single match. Once he had laid bare a weak point, Segura was relentless in his pursuit of the kill. Pancho had the same unique ability to uncover weaknesses in an opponent's arsenal at critical moments of a match.

The greatest combatant the game has ever known, however, did not have to fight to overcome physical shortcomings. Pancho Gonzalez was the complete athlete—tall, strong, lithe and fast. Yet he did not have the bountiful array of superstrokes that other champions possessed. He himself acknowledges that his backhand was often merely defensive and that his forehand could occasionally fold under

pressure. His volleys were not as crisp and decisive as Sedgman's or Laver's, and his training habits were clearly irregular compared to the Spartan regimen of Ken Rosewall. How then, in the face of all these apparent shortcomings, could Gonzalez wind up as a singularly unique champion? One obvious answer is that he possessed the finest serve the game has ever known. But the overriding reason for Pancho's unparalleled success is the fact that he was simply one of the game's outstanding competitors of all time. His competitiveness was not strategically oriented as was Segura's. It was intuitive. Gonzalez was a superlative natural athlete who hated nothing more than defeat. His finest moments in battle were when he radiated belligerence at his foe. Animosity seemed to feed his instincts and when in his famous mood of controlled rage he seldom lost.

*There are fewer upsets among the women than the men. Rosemary Casals*
*(opposite) rarely beats Billie Jean King but will not often lose to*
*anyone ranked below her. W. N'Godrilla (above) is a constant threat.*

# All-Around Athletic Ability

*Ilie Nastase* (above), *despite his bizarre antics on court, is regarded by fellow competitors as having more raw athletic prowess than any other pro in tennis.*

Although no tennis player has ever reached the top ranks of the sport without years of drill, study and exercise, professionals still revere raw athletic ability more than any other quality. They speak reverently of an "athlete," with the silent hope that others will apply the term to them, all the while recognizing that only a handful in the sport's history are entitled to this special sobriquet. Historically, tennis players in general have not been great all-around athletes; that is, a relatively small percentage of tennis players could have excelled in other sports as well. This statement is less true today than it was in the past. Nevertheless, many players of the past—Vines, Perry, Marble, Mulloy, King, Trabert, Emerson and Gonzalez—were marvels of ability.

It is always difficult to compare present-day athletes with those who are no longer active. In some sports—track and field and swimming, for example—concrete timings and measurements tend to discourage debate. In sports such as tennis, however, where seasonal head-to-head competition is the yardstick, a choice of an all-time great is an invitation to controversy.

Most contemporary polls give present-day athletes the edge over their older counterparts on the question of all-around skill. Modern athletes are larger, stronger and faster than those of the past. Swimmers, runners and jumpers improve their times and heights every year. And in the ultimate contest of all-around athletic ability, the Olympic decathalon, the measurable standard of excellence is improved at each outing. It therefore seems reasonable to assume that the best all-around athlete of today is the best of all time.

Having decided that the best athlete in the history of tennis must be selected from a present-day player, one selection becomes easy: Ilie Nastase. He has that rare ability to make moves of magic on court without the spectator being aware that he has done anything special. His rare combination of quickness and anticipation neutralizes a foe's power.

Arthur Ashe articulates the matter succinctly: "Nastase's athletic ability is his best shot."

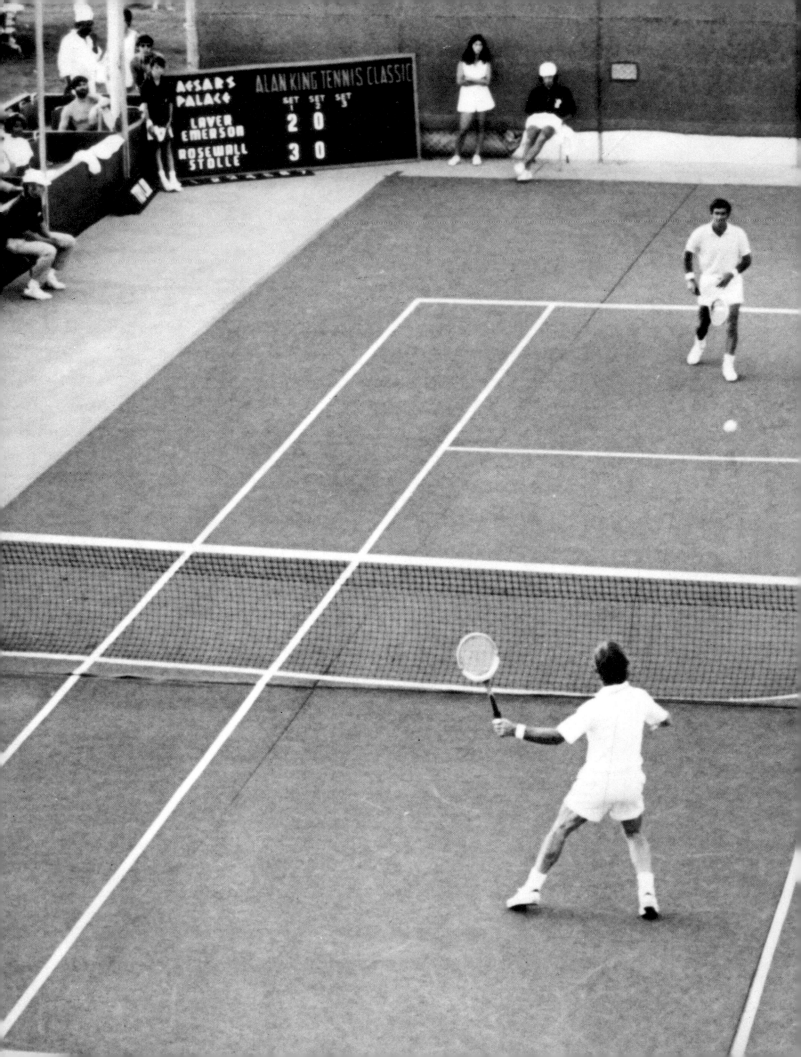

# 5/
# Doubles

Doubles is as different from singles as indoors is from outdoors. The principals are the same, but it is mistakenly assumed that one game is merely an extension of the other. Doubles has a grace and rhythm all its own.

This is not to say that singles champions rarely become doubles champions. On the contrary, any person gifted enough to win the world's most coveted tennis crowns is versatile enough to excel at doubles. The point is that an adjustment must be made to move to the doubles rhythm, an adjustment many players are unwilling to make. For instance, in doubles the ratio of balls hit into the net to balls hit out is three to two. In singles the ratio is even. To understand why is to begin to understand doubles.

A successful doubles partnership must be unselfish. For example, if the net man is lobbed, he has two options after his retrieve: One is to drill the ball, hoping for a spectacular winner; the other is to throw up a defensive lob that will allow time for both him and his partner to reposition themselves. The true doubles mentality subordinates personal satisfaction to the team goal of winning. Though he may have to forsake ego-titillating firepower, the true doubles player resists the impulse for a dramatic ace if the smart percentages call for putting the first serve in play. Sacrifice is vital. In singles, if one misses a daring shot, he alone suffers, and he alone has the chance to recover the lost point. In doubles, the players suffer together, and one of them may not have the opportunity to avenge the lost point himself.

The first innovations in doubles came from men not well-remembered, compared to those whose deeds in singles captivated crowds at Wimbledon or at Forest Hills. In the halcyon days of Major Wingfield, all four players ventured to net only to pick up the balls. C. M. Clark and F. W. Taylor, who won the first U.S. doubles championship at Newport in 1881, experimented by stationing the server's partner at net. This configuration was abandoned when Clark and his brother, Joseph, using the pattern, were crushed at Wimbledon by the Renshaw brothers, who either stayed back or rushed net together. At the turn of the century, the formation of one man at net and the server in backcourt was abandoned completely at the championship level, yet it is still used by club players today. In 1897, the famous Doherty brothers stationed the partner of the service returner at net, planning for the receiver to join his partner for the volley.

Another of the early great doubles players was Holcombe Ward, who won six U.S. titles, from 1899 to 1906. Ward introduced the American twist service. When serving, he threw his toss to the left and slightly in back of his head to produce an exaggerated spin on the ball. His serve would fly in a high, curving arc toward his opponent's backhand and, with sufficient left-to-right spin on the ball, would kick sharply to the right. The delivery was easy to control and gave the server more time to get to the net. It is still the regular serve of most doubles players in the world today. Ward also instituted the tactic of placing the server's partner on the same side of the court as the server, to defend against a strong cross-court return of service. Utilized most by the Australians, the position was tagged "the Australian formation," and is still used today, although the standard position remains partner on opposite side of server.

The first brilliant doubles force was R. Norris Williams and Vincent Richards, who were unbeaten in major competition from 1925 to 1926. Some consider them the greatest combination in tennis history. They combined all the elements of good doubles—consistent return of serve, dominance at net, adroit use of angles—that had been separately developed by others.

Louise Brough and Margaret Osborne DuPont won 12 U.S. Nationals, five Wimbledons and three championships of France, part of a never-equaled, never-threatened record of 20 major titles. Neither woman blazed with speed, but each complemented the other at net with flawless teamwork. They honed to perfection the "dink," the gently chipped return of service to the feet of the net rusher. Brough and DuPont each found individuality in winning without trying to be a star.

William F. Talbert and Gardner Mulloy, winners of four U.S. Nationals titles, were direct descendants of the Williams–Richards style of play. Neither Mulloy nor Talbert were exponents of power, but both could use it as a change of pace. Talbert would gently pick the angles, and Mulloy would suddenly follow with a forehand thunderclap up the middle.

Adrian Quist and John Bromwich won their native Australian doubles championships for eight

Preceding pages: *Rosewall and Stolle in the backcourt and Laver and Emerson at net, four reasons for recent Australian doubles dominance.* Opposite top: *Orantes and Nastase.* Opposite bottom: *Lesley Hunt joins partner Evonne Goolagong at net.*

consecutive years. They made their fortune with consistency in the backcourt and acutely angled shots at net. Also, they added a dimension to the dink by following the chipped return to net. For quickness at the net, however, none could match Aussies Frank Sedgman and Ken McGregor, who scored impressive Wimbledon and Davis Cup triumphs in 1951 and 1952. McGregor, tall as an oak, answered any desperation lob intended to push the pair away from the net with lethal overhead firings.

Normally, it takes many years for a doubles combination to develop the teamwork and understanding necessary to be consistently successful. The lone exception was Ken Rosewall and Lew Hoad, who, as 18-year-olds, won the 1953 Wimbledon, Australian and French doubles championships. Rosewall's magical backhand, which could thread winners through the tiniest openings, was the perfect foil for Hoad's imposing presence at the net. This team developed the "drift"—the net man of the receiving side intercepting the server's volley. Classically, Rosewall would stroke a firm, backhand angle return of service, and Hoad, in the deuce court, would move to the middle to intercept the server's volley.

An interception by the server's net man is called a "poach." The origin of the poach is uncertain, but it is known that both English and American tandems experimented with it before 1900. The triumphs of Vic Seixas and Tony Trabert in the 1953 and 1954 Davis Cup Challenge Rounds were largely attributed to their planned use of the poach. Before each point, Trabert would turn to Seixas and let him know by hand signal whether or not he would cross. John Newcombe and Tony Roche are a modern team that has combined the poach and the drift well—they have captured four recent Wimbledon titles. They concentrate their guard at the center of the court rather than at the sides, where the net is higher. This "packing the center" was a strategy developed by Australian teams in the early 1950s.

Though a great doubles player does not create the excitement of a great doubles team, there are a legion of players who excelled with many different partners. Roy Emerson has one of the most consistent doubles records, having collected two Wimbledon, three Australian, four U.S. Nationals and six French triumphs. Billie Jean King, with seven Wimbledon crowns, is an exceptional doubles

*The irony of doubles is that although it is preferred by the overwhelming majority of weekend players, prize money of professional tournaments emphasizes singles to please the sponsors and ignores good doubles teams.*

player, as is Margaret Court, with three Wimbledon, three French, five U.S. and six Australian victories to her credit. Elizabeth Ryan established the most impressive list of all, 19 Wimbledon titles with myriad partners, although she never won the singles.

In forming a doubles combination psychological pairing is as important as matching complementary strokes. Doubles demands constant off-court adjustment as well as on-court teamwork. The well-recognized "cabin fever," the malady that comes with grating, close personal contact in highly competitive situations, can destroy any doubles pairing. Often the psychological strain becomes monstrous after a few frustrating losses, and the team splits up. However, when an old pairing separates (as Romanians Ilie Nastase and Ian Tiriac did in 1972) and comes back together, the renewal may bring new excitement and creation. When Bob Lutz

joined Lamar Hunt's tour, the awesome team of Stan Smith and Lutz, the only U.S. team to have won three Challenge Round doubles, appeared on the verge of collapse. Now that all professionals can compete together, it is likely that Smith and Lutz will come together and form their potent combination once again.

To better understand the ingredients necessary for an outstanding partnership, one must review the patterns of the great teams. Rarely have players of the same style performed well together. Successful pairings usually featured a playmaker, one who was steady enough to keep the ball in play until his partner could execute the killing volley. Bromwich was such a quarterback for Quist, Talbert for Mulloy, Rosewall for Hoad. Sometimes the roles switched, especially when both partners were power proponents. The styles of Sedgman and McGregor were similar, as were those of Newcombe and

Above: *Margaret Court runs to retrieve a lob hit over the head of partner Virginia Wade. Though Court and Wade are excellent doubles players, they do not have a regular partnership such as Casals and King do (opposite).*

Roche, Smith and Lutz. Each of these men could thunder every ball, yet would select the best blend of tennis ingredients for the match at hand.

The elements of that blend are not always obvious. One may happen on success through a lucky service return that puffs one player's pride so much that he refuses to miss. He becomes the steady playmaker for that match. Regardless of the players' roles on any day, success always demands individual sacrifice for the team.

More than diplomacy suggests that top mixed doubles depends more on the woman than on the man. Recalling Wimbledon and U.S. mixed champions of the past 30 years, one finds that often the women partners also won the singles the same year. The best woman can pick almost any partner and win the mixed, perhaps because many of the best men refuse to play the mixed. The cash prize isn't significant, and the preparation can foul up their training schedule for the singles.

As world rankings and prize money today concentrate on the singles player, doubles, sadly, takes a backseat. The style of doubles play, for example, has been dramatically affected. Defense has been abandoned in favor of attack. The reason is simple. If the doubles partner has a singles match the next day, subconsciously he practices for that match, using the shots he will need in singles. If he concentrated on defense, the match might protract into a lobbing, dinking and retrieving contest that could tire him for the following day's critical singles. With caution discarded in doubles, there are more spectacular shots but, also, fewer prolonged, tension-building rallies.

The unique features of doubles makes it an excellent weekender's sport as well as an enthralling spectator event. With the tennis court conveniently carved in half, it is easier for older players to cover their area. Still, top professionals playing doubles can fire snappy net exchanges, dynamic in their kaleidoscopic patterns. Doubles is the sophisticated older brother of singles. It is the form for which tennis was conceived. Unfortunately, at the professional level, doubles has been relegated to a sideshow status, although at most clubs and public parks players engage in doubles only. Perhaps doubles will return as a professional spectacle. Television, the older pros and the weekenders may demand it.

*Teamwork in doubles is an elusive quality. Not only must the physical talents of the pair be complementary, but elements of respect, friendship, and comraderie will make the tandem function much more efficiently.*

# The Forums 6/

Contrary to popular conception, all tennis courts are not the same; in no other sport do different playing surfaces mean as much as they do in tennis. John Newcombe can win on Wimbledon's grass and be proclaimed the world's best player, only to lose to Istvan Gulyas, a 40-year-old Hungarian, the next week on the slow clay at Gstaad. Europeans thrive on slow clay courts, where power is less important than finesse and conditioning. The ball used in Europe is slightly spongier than that used in England or America, producing interminable rallies, which hamper the power player. In Rome or Paris, Australians bash their service, and the ball floats limply back. The speed of a crisp volley is absorbed both by the ball and the court, leaving an exuberant net rusher cringing in the wake of a well-placed return of his best shot. Naturally, players excel on the surface most familiar to them—Australians on grass, Europeans on clay, Californians on cement, Swedes indoors. Only rarely does a champion perform well on all surfaces.

With one exception, the forums described herein are unique in tradition and international character and offer either big prize money or a high caliber of competition. Only Melbourne's Kooyong is a suspect choice. Kooyong is no more renowned than White City Stadium in Sydney or Memorial Stadium in Adelaide, but we chose it as a representative forum for all Australia. The site of the Aussie Nationals alternates each year, with the result that no Australian forum is preeminent. Yet it is felt that collectively the arenas at Perth, Brisbane, Sydney, Adelaide and Melbourne deserve discussion.

# Kooyong

For centuries, aborigines honed their hunting skills at Kooyong, "the Haunt of the Wild Fowl," a three-sided basin on the southeastern tip of Australia. Though the protagonists and their purposes differ, the hunt continues today on the same site. In January, champion tennis players gather at the underside of the globe to contest the first jewel of the famed Grand Slam (the Australian, French, Wimbledon and U.S. titles). The prestige of the Australian Nationals has diminished with the crush of enormous prize money offered elsewhere, sums that

*Kooyong's stadium occupies three of the ground's forty acres. Stadium courts are constructed beneath ground level, and capacity now is 13,000 people.*

the Aussies cannot match. But as certain as it was that tribesmen would return to Kooyong to hunt a millenium ago, the glory of tennis staged in Australia will be restored.

Kooyong is on the outskirts of Melbourne, birthplace of the Australian Lawn Tennis Association and Harry Hopman, the sage Davis Cup coach for more than 20 years, who lost but a handful of Challenge Rounds. Seventeen acres of gentle, rustic land surround the horseshoe-shaped stadium, which encloses 3 of the 40 courts on the grounds. Seasonal flowers, rock gardens, trees and tiny pathways lend a full-day-outing atmosphere for the casually dressed Melbourne spectator. Bermuda shorts and micro-mini skirts reflect the carefree character of tennis fans here, and inexpensive ticket prices ($1.10 $3.50) encourage the whole family to come.

The venerable architectural firm of Bates, Smart and McCutcheon designed the stadium, in 1932, so that spectators entered on ground level

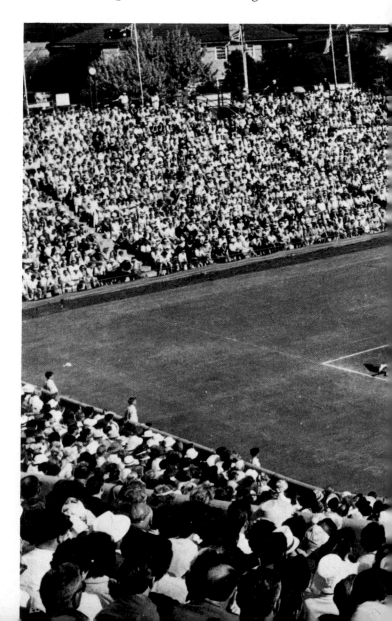

and looked down on the center court at subground level. As overflow crowds cheered thunderously for whiz kids Rosewall and Hoad from 1953 to 1956, more seats were needed. Additional tiers gave the complex an erector-set appearance, but they increased capacity to almost 13,000. Unlike the cold bastion of White City, the subground-level courts at Kooyong give the pros the feeling of playing amidst, not merely before, the large galleries.

Aussie grass is different from the lushness of Wimbledon or the brittleness of Forest Hills. It is low and as hard as a roadbed, producing lightning-fast but flawless bounces. The Meeri Creek river irrigates the soil that produces Kooyong's green, the equal of turf anywhere. A sturdy combination of Kentucky blue, rye and creeping bent, the turf is almost indestructible, even to a determined toe-dragger. By April, the end of the tennis season, the courts are worn and soiled to a green-brown stubble that resembles a three-day beard. Nonetheless, the

surface stays even and gives a true bounce, even after a succession of tournaments. The surface is as hard as cement, but there are still no ruts. At Forest Hills, because of a weak subsoil, the courts become spongelike after the first rain. There, a ball's first bounce is likely to be its last. But after a deluge at Kooyong, the rich river earth combines with the rain to form a pastelike mud. As the grounds dry, they can be rolled and manicured into the same resilient, even pitch as before.

Australians are wizards on grass. Roy Emerson, with a record seven Aussie titles to his credit, must be considered the greatest magician of all. The Melbourne courts are perfect for Emerson's footwork.

Summer in Australia runs from November to April. Summer temperatures in Melbourne are moderate, ranging from 70 to 90 degrees, which makes Kooyong more popular with professionals than the tropical temperature extremes of the Milton Courts at Brisbane or the irregular climate of White City.

# Forest Hills

Tennis is one of the few sports whose arenas do not separate the spectator and his champion with screens or concrete. Baseball, football, basketball and soccer have segregated the player from his supporters, in some instances by a water-filled moat. But in tennis, even the bastions of Forest Hills, Wimbledon and Roland Garros are tempered by a field-court arrangement, where players can mingle with their fans before early-round matches. Nowhere do the spectators take better advantage of this convenient layout than at Forest Hills.

Armed with stapled schedules, spectators jam the narrow, chair-lined aisles during the early rounds of the United States Open. Some ensconce themselves for an entire match, others watch a single set before scurrying off to catch a glimpse of old favorites or to watch a particularly interesting match on a clubhouse court. Such a garden-party atmosphere, when not a function of snobbery, helps to convert the spectators into participants.

Only Wimbledon is older than the U.S. National Championships. The U.S. Championships was first held at the stodgy Casino Club in Newport, Rhode Island, in the fall of 1881. Proper dress for the men players included neckties, and both men and women wore brimmed hats to shield them from the sun. Richard Sears, 19 years old, won the first event at Newport, over a field of 25. He repeated six times before retiring undefeated. In 1887, at the Philadelphia Cricket Club, the ladies held their first championship. Ellen Hansell won the first final over Laura Knight, 6–1, 6–0. Both girls wore long dresses, equally long slips and diaphanous hats that tied under their chins.

Five years later, in New York City's Central Park, 13 players formed the West Side Tennis Club. The grounds were four dirt courts. As interest in tennis increased, the club twice moved farther uptown to accommodate its growing membership. In 1913, the club purchased its present 11-acre site in Forest Hills, Queens, built a clubhouse and laid out 23 clay and 22 grass courts. The Nationals continued at Newport from 1915 to 1920 when it moved to Forest Hills, after which it was hosted briefly by the Germantown Cricket Club in Philadelphia. But the fathers of the United States Lawn Tennis Associa-

*The West Side Tennis Club in Forest Hills, New York, has a field-court arrangement, which allows spectators to mingle with players as they scurry from match to match. Fans, like their dress, are casual.*

tion (USLTA) had had their eye on the West Side Tennis Club since 1914, when it had staged a Davis Cup Challenge Round between Australia and the United States at Forest Hills before 14,000 fans stacked in temporary wooden stands. In 1923, West Side constructed the present stadium, which seats almost 15,000, and a year later, the U.S. Nationals made their home there. Despite its imposing concrete horseshoe facade, the Forest Hills Stadium is a friendly setting for American tennis. Tournament chairman Bill Talbert, who as a player roamed the grounds in glory decades earlier, has added walkways so that spectators can amble amidst the endless field courts and mingle with the players.

With a change in international amateur rules in 1968, Forest Hills became an Open. The same year, with the professional players came professional promoters. Madison Square Garden lent advice. In 1969, South African Owen Williams became the Open's first professional tournament director. Ticket prices now scale to a $9 top, a hot dog costs 45 cents and the end of the spiral is not in sight.

Because the United States hasn't the same regard for tradition as Wimbledon, the grounds on which the U.S. Championships is held are not considered sacred. As bids from California threaten to move the Nationals to Los Angeles, the pros continually complain about the uneven turf at the West Side. The grass there has subsoil problems that cause the pitch to become uneven after a heavy rain. Two improvisations may preserve the site—one, to enclose the open end of the horseshoe with a modern glass-enveloped structure, the other, to experiment with either Har Tru composition or synthetic courts to replace the grass. But if the lawn is removed at Forest Hills, grass will be gone forever from top-flight American tennis, which now stages preliminary events on Eastern turf only so that the pros can prepare for Forest Hills and the U.S. Open.

174

*Field courts afford the spectators a view from only*
*one angle, but youths, many of whom have somehow managed to*
*avoid paying, find other places from which to watch.*

# Ellis Park

In the great forums, tradition, competition and prize money transcend the importance of any one man—except at Ellis Park in Johannesburg. Ellis Park and professional tennis in South Africa have, in large part, been created by local entrepreneur Owen Williams. The stadium was built in 1923 on an unused brickyard. Originally, the rectangular arena consisted of two center courts enclosed by a covered stand on the north end and three open stands. Today an entirely covered stadium that seats 6,000 surrounds one center count. The complex of 20 courts within the park grounds seats an additional 4,000.

With great foresight, Williams built an elegant Tennis Patrons' Club in 1964, at a cost of more than $200,000, an unheard of expense when the game's promotional potential seemed limited. Williams, the world's first international tennis promoter, placed special emphasis on spectator comfort. The club has a luxurious box that overlooks the center court and a glass-enclosed viewing area from which one can observe the outside courts. Though the atmosphere is elegant, tickets are modestly priced, from 1 to 5 rand (one rand equals $1.25).

The surface for all courts is cement. With today's emphasis on maintenance-free, all-weather surfaces, it is unusual that Ellis Park is the only international fixture with cement. The surface selection, however, was more necessity than choice. Torrid days of 110 degrees under a baking sun, alternating with torrential downpours, would have destroyed any surface other than cement.

The distinguishing characteristic of this hard court is its near-perfect but fast bounce. Since Johannesburg has an elevation of more than 2,000 feet, the ball fires through the thin air like a gunshot and is difficult to control. Californians Ralston, Ashe and Smith are the kind of players who would perform well at Ellis Park. The servers and volleyers have an advantage over strict baseliners, though Richey and Santana have won the South African Nationals by relying on heavily topspinned groundstrokes. Though its economic and practical qualities are apparent, cement is an unyielding, uncomfortable surface. But at Ellis Park, the emphasis is on the spectator and his comfort, not on the players, who resemble gladiators.

176

*Built in 1923, Ellis Park in South Africa is the only
international fixture on cement. The combination
of 100-degree temperatures and torrential rain would ruin other surfaces.*

# Foro Italico

Foro Italico is auspiciously close to the historic Coliseum in Rome and, fittingly, is the only stadium more heralded than its winners. Playing before an Italian crowd at the "Foro" is a theatrical experience remembered for a lifetime.

The stadium complex was constructed in 1925 and encloses six courts in two-court sections. With local pine trees separating each tier and potted plants and window boxes as trimming, Foro Italico is the most serene setting in all tennis—except when the Italian Championships is staged in May. Then, the Foro explodes in patriotic frenzy as Italian stars perform. Ringing chants of *"Die Fausto," "Die Nicola"* or *"Die Adriano"* stir local heroes to the miraculous. They receive less-spiritual assistance too. The clay surface topped with a red brick dust, and the soft Pirelli ball that slows rallies to a standstill have felled more than one tennis giant. Countless Americans and Australians, armed with monstrous serves and volleys, have been brought to their knees at Foro Italico.

The stands at the number one and two courts seat approximately 5,000 people. Those for the remaining four courts accommodate another 5,000. Tickets are inexpensive at 1,000 lire each (approximately $2) except those for the exclusive club parapet, with its large picture windows overlooking the main arena. Sun and space are omnipresent. Carefully kept grass aisles separate the cement tiers on which the spectators sit. Tall, Umbrian trees surround the courts like sentinels, their task to ensure that no matter how frantic the crowd becomes, Roman order will prevail.

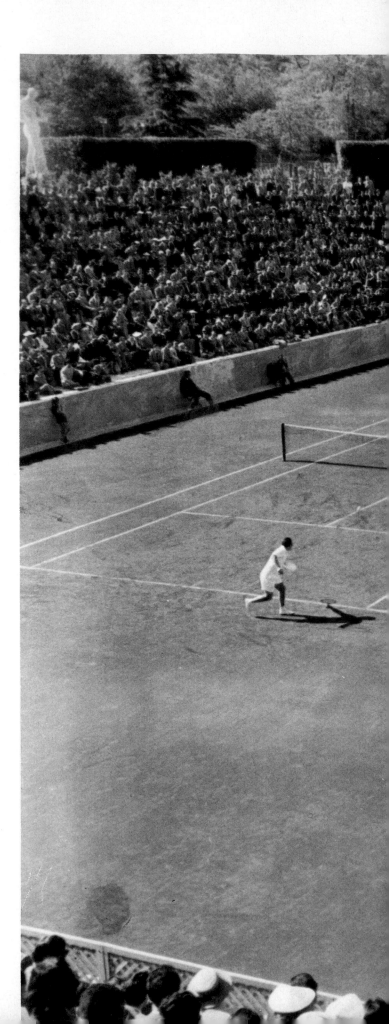

*Typically Roman, the six courts of Foro Italico are surrounded by pine trees, potted plants and statuary. While the setting is serene, the crowds are not.*

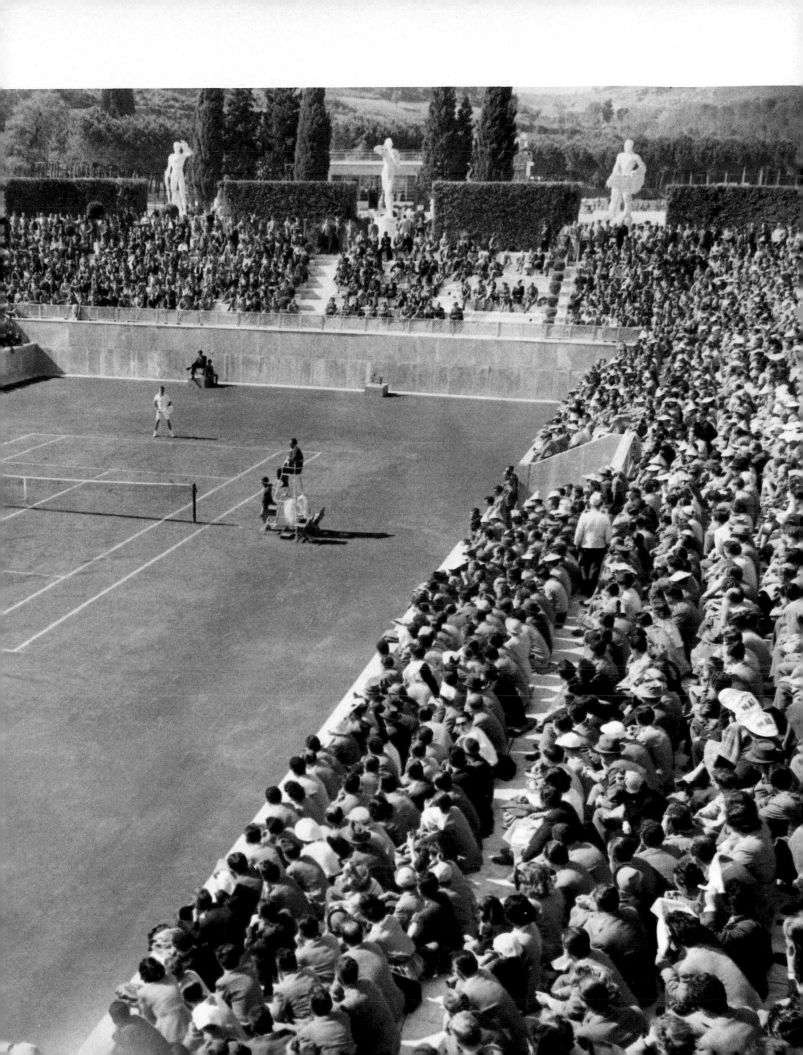

# Roland Garros

Le Stade Roland Garros is a French monument to four athletes. In contrast to Foro Italico in Rome, the tradition of Roland Garros is people. The stadium was built in response to public frenzy over René LaCoste, Henri Cochet, Jean Borotra and Jacques Brugnon, the legendary "four musketeers" who, in 1927, upset the American Davis Cup team of Bill Tilden and Billy Johnston. The French had to defend the Cup the following year, but there was no arena large enough for the hero-worshiping fans. Roland Garros was built the next spring in Porte d'Auteil, an elegant Paris suburb. Today, the concrete structure seats 14,000 around a single center court, while other matches are contested outside on 10 field courts. The fabled arena was named after a spirited First World War aviator, who was killed in 1918 in an epic air battle.

French fans are fanatic in support of their countrymen's exploits. The slow red clay courts have frustrated all but the most fearless attacking foreigners. Indeed, Frenchmen won these famous Championships exclusively for 41 years, from 1891 to 1933, until Aussie Jack Crawford broke the natives' reign. The legendary Suzanne Lenglen, with six triumphs, helped keep the women's title strictly French for 26 years. But athletes from overseas have since recovered their lost honor. In the past 45 years, only two French men and four French women have won the Championships. Finally, after a 19-year famine, France ascended again when the unorthodox Francoise Durr captured the crown in 1967 and became an overnight celebrity.

The French have always felt more strongly about the players who contested their Championships than about mere stiff and obscure tradition. Despite their patriotism, the French collect substitute heroes from the foreign warriors who repeat triumphs in their event. Professionals are unanimous in considering the French Championships the toughest in the world to win just once, so grueling are the three-of-five-set matches on the quicksand clay courts. Among the special group who have triumphed twice, the French feel special affection for Drobney, Trabert, Pietrangeli and Santana, men whose dramatic personalities projected vividly to the crowd. And a unique amour is reserved for Australian Ken Rosewall, who first won at Paris in 1953 at

age 18 and returned years later to triumph at 33. Never has there been a greater span between victories than between those the proud Rosewall produced.

Only one month favorably compares with April in Paris—May in Paris. Local fauna, countless trees in many shapes, bright sunshine and lithe sportsmen who bound around the courts make an afternoon at Roland Garros glorious. Ticket prices from 20 to

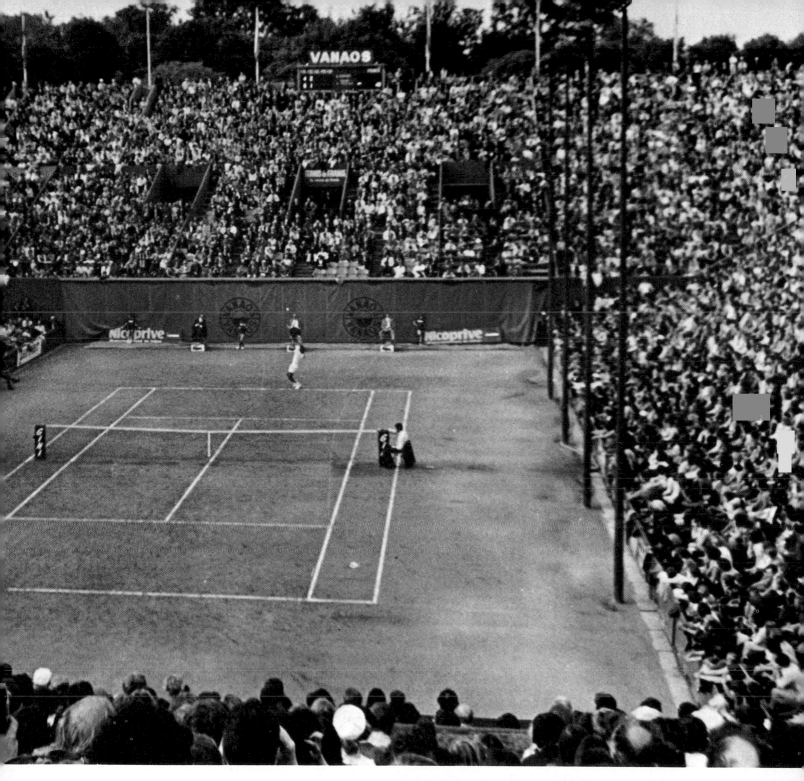

40 francs ($4 to $8) are expensive, but so is everything else in Paris.

Tennis as we know it originated in thirteenth-century French monasteries, and the game here hasn't changed much. The incantation in French of the score, *"egalité"* or *"quinze par tous,"* is the same as it was 700 years ago. Roland Garros looks to its legends, the swashbuckling musketeers and the double winners.

*Roland Garros was built in 1928 for the thousands of French tennis enthusiasts who demanded the right to see the "four musketeers" in action. Ten field courts surround a single center court around which 14,000 fans can be seated at prices ranging from $4 to $8.*

# Dallas

Only Texas could develop tradition overnight. The Moody Coliseum, the simple Southern Methodist University gymnasium, was constructed in the suburbs of Dallas in 1956. It's a typically undistinguished building in the lackluster style of hundreds of other campus athletic facilities. But in 1971 and 1972, Moody became the forum for the richest tournament in tennis history, called, perhaps presumptuously, "the World Championship of Tennis."

Modern tennis is gall and presumption based on the brashness of the big buck, and the metamorphosis of Moody from shapeless pumpkin to Cinderella's majestic carriage was easy. Add blue bunting, a synthetic-carpet playing surface, the ecstasy of 8,500 fans, the less audible frenzy of 21 million in TV land, eight of the world's best tennis players, a first prize of $50,000 and, zap, instant tradition. Texas oilman Lamar Hunt, whose other expensive sports hobbies include the Kansas City Chiefs (football) and the Dallas Tornado (soccer), waved the magic wand and made the transformation.

The choice of Moody Coliseum as the site for one of the world's most important tennis tournaments symbolizes the game's direction. Tennis is big business. Scheduling and logistics are of paramount importance. Promoters need to know which stars can participate, how much money to offer and when to stage the grand finale. Weather, of course, will not interfere.

Hunt selected the eight best players in a worldwide tournament that was heresy to a traditionalist. The eight were spit from a computer, having been graded in a series of 20 WCT worldwide tournaments. Thus, the promoter was ensured a year in advance of top performers, insurance that, in the vagaries of tennis politics, had previously been

impossible. The date for the final showdown was also scheduled a year in advance—once again, an obvious but revolutionary tactic in a game that traditionally waits until the last moment to fix the time and place for any championship.

Some of the innovations at Moody Coliseum were not Hunt's, but he instituted them anyway. He used the tie-breaker to avert long, dreary matches. He ordered a green carpet surface, untraditional to be sure but conducive to long rallies and

*Lamar Hunt* (below) *created instant tradition when his $50,000 World Championship of Tennis finals became a spectacular tournament in only two years. The forum is Southern Methodist University's Moody Coliseum, which is indoors and features a synthetic playing surface.*

very fine for players and spectators alike to look at.

In May, 1972, Ken Rosewall and Rod Laver dueled in the finals of the World Championship of Tennis. It was later called the finest match ever played. Certainly, it was played before the largest tennis television audience in history. There will be improvements in scheduling, scoring and surfaces, but for now, Hunt has fused the necessary elements for a major sports spectacle. And the Moody Coliseum is the forum.

# Wimbledon

The world's oldest, most prestigious tennis tournament is formally called the Lawn Tennis Championships on Grass. In 1877, Englishman Spencer Gore won the men's singles over a field that totaled just 22. Today, there are 128 entries in men's singles, 96 in women's singles, 64 pairs in men's doubles, 48 pairs in women's doubles and 80 teams in mixed doubles.

It is unusual for the oldest of anything to still be the best, but Wimbledon is. It has changed to keep pace with and even ahead of the times. In 1968, it was the first tennis event to accept both amateurs and professionals, in defiance of a century-old international edict against open tennis. The tournament is administered the year round, facilitating the planning and allowing changes to be made gradually.

Add to the mechanical smoothness the glitter of Wimbledon—roses and hydrangeas, fresh strawberries and cream served at doll-house kiosks, players arriving in long black limousines, endless ivy—and one gets an impression of the ultimate spectacle. But to feel the tradition that suffuses the All-England Lawn Tennis and Croquet Club, one must visit there probably more than once. Perhaps after a half-dozen times roaming the grounds one can begin to understand this tennis spectacle.

There are 8 hard (clay) courts, 2 indoor courts and 15 grass courts, where the Championships are played. Though the present stadium was built in 1922, the grounds can accommodate 30,000 fans—more than any other tennis facility in the world. Actually, Wimbledon is a handful of stadiums. Almost 1,000 fans can observe play on the number three court, almost 3,000 on the number two court and nearly 8,000 on the number one court. But the hoopla surrounds the famed Centre Court, around which 15,000 jammed to see the 1972 Nastase-Smith final. Sacred to its players, the Centre Court is respected, feared, hallowed. Opponents are hustled into waiting rooms before each match so that their scene on this famed tennis stage will begin punctually.

Head groundsman Robert Twynan keeps a diary on the condition of the one-fifth acre that is

the Centre Court. Each day, he inspects the grass with a jeweler's eye, and he frequently falls on hands and knees to rid the glorious lawn of the weeds British groundsmen call "volunteers." The dominant species of grass is Dutch highlight chewing fescue mixed with a small dose of Oregon browntop, an American grass. Twynan subjects the grass to a number of horticultural heresies. Most groundsmen roll turf only occasionally, and then with a light roller. Twynan regularly pounds his grass with a 2,500-pound roller.

Grass is roundly criticized for its irregular bounce and unfair partiality toward serves. But while others replace their grass, Wimbledon and Twynan persevere. Players consider Wimbledon's the finest grass in the world. Wimbledon will always have its velvet lawns, immune from criticism by all but the blasphemous.

The competitor's tearoom at Wimbledon is up a flight of stairs, next to the number-one court's north facade. Inside, tournament negotiations take place for that season and part of the next. Substitute ticker tape for the recorded match results

*The Lawn Tennis Championships on Grass, better known as Wimbledon, is the world's most prestigious tournament. The grounds—eight clay courts, two indoor courts, fifteen grass courts—accommodate 30,000 people.*

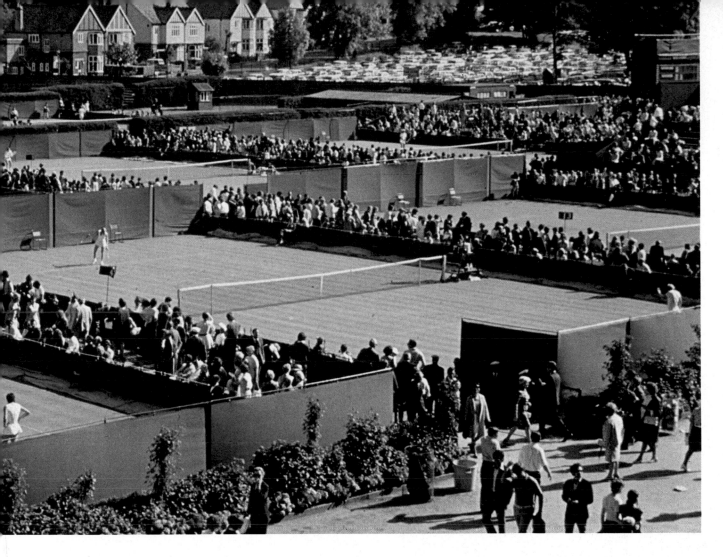

and grand prix standings, which are in full view of every tearoom window, and the scene could be the New York Stock Exchange. The official tennis peace will soon make contracts obsolete and restore serenity to the tearoom. Already tournament negotiations are less important than a few years ago, because now Lamar Hunt's contract pros have to play where they are told. Still, most official business today is transacted in this room. Wimbledon remains the focus of tennis political activity. For example, the International Lawn Tennis Federation and the Davis Cup nations meet during the Wimbledon fortnight.

Wimbledon is many things to the players who have played there and to the spectators who have watched. It is more than observing an ace dramatically raise the finely pulverized chalk on the service line. It is an experience as bracing as British rain.

The Championships, as the English say, leaving no doubt what they mean, is both the official meeting place for the top brass and the reunion ground for former players, from officials to those of the inner tennis family, who congregate once a year in

London to talk tennis and relive their memories. The veterans' doubles, an event for players over 45, best demonstrates the Wimbledon tradition. The elderly competitors receive the same amenities, including chauffeur-driven limousines and choice tickets for friends, as the top stars. But while all competitors are treated equally, some are treated more equally than others. Champions needn't contend with the "B" dressing room, smaller and with fewer showers and trainers than the spacious, elegant "A" locker room, and champions are accorded privileges not given lesser men. Each year's men's champion becomes a lifetime honorary member of the All-England Club, no small honor, considering that there are only 375 regular members.

The stadium at Wimbledon may one day be rebuilt to satisfy modern stadium tastes or to placate the local safety marshal, who now can rely only on the Deity to ward off fire in the giant wooden tinderbox that encloses the Centre Court.

But if the ancient structure is removed, the echo of tradition will remain. The stadium is at once both Wimbledon and tennis itself.

7/

# Luck of the Draw

Are today's stars superior to those of yesteryear? In that endless, monotonous argument, the imponderables are large. What surface would be chosen? Would modern equipment be used by old-timers, or would Arthur Ashe have to serve with a spoon-shaped wooden relic? Would Tilden alter his serving and volleying style? Could Helen Wills handle Billie Jean King's bustle about the court? Such absurd conjecture might be stilled if 32 of the best men and 16 of the best women in tennis history were to come together in the same tournament. And the tourney's outcome might be dictated by the draw.

In every championship tennis event, the tournament committee selects at least eight of the best players, a selection based on the players' recent performance. These elite players are called "seeds" and are separated in the draw so that they will not meet, if form holds true, until the quarterfinals. (The reason for seeding is obvious. It would be disastrous if the best players were to eliminate each other in the opening rounds, leaving one good player and seven rabbits in the quarterfinals.) After the seeds are placed in the draw, the names of the remaining players are picked by chance to determine pairings. To give tradition its due, the names in our super championship were paired by drawing them from the Davis Cup itself, before it was sent into sacred storage in Tiffany's vaults. We trust the more stringent traditionalists will not be disconcerted by the thought of tennis generations united in the great urn.

When people attempt to rate the all-time great players, they usually fail to realize that tennis is a game of distinct match-ups in which the pairings are as important as an accurate first serve. Rod Laver has beaten Arthur Ashe 12 times without losing. With almost as much regularity, Ashe defeats Marty Riessen, yet Riessen gives fits to Laver. He has won at least half their meetings. Match-ups can present psychological subplots, which have nothing to do with tactics or skill but which can affect the outcome of the contest just as much. Ashe, for example, rose through the junior ranks considering Riessen, though only 16 months older, a journeyman player with solid but not exceptional skills. In later years, Ashe could not alter his original impression, even after Riessen radically supercharged his game. With such confidence, Ashe dominated their meetings. When players have similar or offsetting skills, as they do on the top professional level, confidence is crucial. Any super championship, therefore, will be affected by the draw, which can determine match-ups that psychologically unhinge one player or arouse confidence in another. Stan Smith would have had an excellent chance of upsetting Bill Tilden, so mechanically perfect and basic are Smith's serve and volley. But Smith would have been baffled by the athleticism of Tony Trabert, who, in turn, would have been bedeviled by Henri Cochet's guile. Unmindful of such psychological factors, many Davis Cup captains choose their teams in challenge matches with little regard for who the opposition will be. Smith might lose to Tom Gorman in intrasquad competition, but Gorman, having never beaten Ilie Nastase, would be a poor choice to face the agile Romanian. The surface is also important. In the championship, we envisioned a surface with enough traction to help the fleet and one that produced the ideal bounces—fast

Pancho Gonzalez.

NAME

1. Bill Tilden
Tilden
(2–6, 3–6, 6–4, 6–4, 6–4)
2. Vic Seixas
Tilden
(2–6, 3–6, 6–4, 6–4, 6–4)
3. Arthur Ashe
Ashe
(4–6, 6–2, 6–3, 6–4)
4. Maurice McLaughlin
Tilden
(6–4, 6–2, 2–6, 2–6, 7–6)
5. Chuck McKinley
Rosewall
(2–6, 6–4, 6–3, 6–4)
6. Ken Rosewall
LaCoste
(6–4, 4–6, 6–2, 1–6, 6–2)
7. René LaCoste
LaCoste
(4–6, 6–3, 6–2, 7–6)
8. Tony Roche
Gonzalez
(3–6, 6–2, 6–3, 6–4)
9. Bobby Riggs
Perry
(1–6, 6–4, 6–2, 5–7, 7–6)
10. Fred Perry
Perry
(7–5, 6–7, 7–5, 6–7, 7–5)
11. Stan Smith
Smith
(6–4, 6–3, 2–6, 7–6)
12. Frank Sedgman
Gonzalez
(6–3, 7–5, 7–6)
13. Lew Hoad
Hoad
(3–6, 6–4, 6–2, 6–3)
14. Bill Johnston
Gonzalez
(1–6, 7–6, 2–6, 6–4, 7–6)
15. Pancho Gonzalez
Gonzalez
(1–6, 2–6, 6–3, 6–4, 6–2)
16. Ellsworth Vines
Gonzalez
(6–3, 7–5, 7–6)
17. Don Budge
Budge
(6–2, 7–5, 7–6)
18. Alex Olmedo
Budge
(7–5, 6–4, 6–4)
19. Roy Emerson
Emerson
(2–6, 4–6, 6–4, 6–4, 7–5)
20. Frank Parker
Budge
(3–6, 4–6, 6–4, 7–5, 7–6)
21. Jean Borotra
Nastase
(0–4, 0–0, 0–4, 7–6)
22. Ilie Nastase
Kramer
(2–6, 7–5, 6–4, 6–3)
23. Jack Kramer
Kramer
(7–5, 6–4, 6–2)
24. R. F. Doherty
Laver
(6–4, 6–4, 2–6, 7–6)
25. Henri Cochet
Cochet
(0–6, 6–1, 0–6, 6–4, 7–6)
26. Manuel Santana
Cochet
(6–4, 2–6, 6–4, 6–3)
27. Richard Sears
Newcombe
(2–6, 6–4, 7–6, 7–6)
28. John Newcombe
Laver
(6–4, 6–4, 2–6, 7–6)
29. Anthony E. Wilding
Trabert
(7–5, 7–5, 7–5)
30. Tony Trabert
Laver
(4–6, 6–4, 7–5, 6–7, 6–3)
31. H. L. Doherty
Laver
(6–1, 6–4, 7–6)
32. Rod Laver

SEEDED PLAYERS

1. Tilden
2. Laver
3. Budge
4. Gonzalez
5. Kramer
6. LaCoste
7. Perry
8. Cochet

enough to give a premium for boldness, true enough to ensure errorless rallies. In short, we assumed the ideal surface. We picked Pancho Gonzalez to win. As often as not, Lew Hoad might beat Gonzalez, but we picked Pancho to prevail in an arduous tournament.

The best match of the first round was Nastase–Borotra, a pairing of fidgety, high-strung temperaments. Nastase won when his bustle bewildered the frenetic Frenchman.

Ashe defeated Maurice McLaughlin, his first opponent, in a battle of whistling serves. Cochet outlasted Manuel Santana, in a triumph of cunning over artistry. John Newcombe's firepower overwhelmed Dick Sears. Smith's basic speed of service offset Frank Sedgman's quickness at net, and Gonzalez, though outshot by the talented Ellsworth Vines, was the more resolute competitor.

In the second round, the Tilden–Ashe affair was the most intriguing as "Big Bill" dropped the first two sets, as was his custom, but accelerated dramatically to win the next three, by identical scores, 6–4. Trabert performed with customary, all-American heroics before bowing to Laver. Fred Perry taunted Smith for his implacable seriousness, making Smith a sentimental choice, but Perry's athletic facility conquered Smith, whose concentration was nonetheless exemplary, particularly when he won both sudden-death sets. In a match of service bombardments, Gonzalez won over Hoad with competitive brilliance at crisis.

In the quarterfinals, Gonzalez's toughness was the proper riposte to Perry's raw tongue and raw talent, but Tilden's win over René LaCoste came only with a flicker of luck—he served the last of the sudden-death points. Laver's powerful wrists produced mighty topspin on both forehand and back-

hand, and dispirited Cochet. Budge and Kramer, unluckily placed in the same sector of the draw, resolved the issue when Budge bludgeoned a winning backhand return of Kramer's second serve in the final point of the tie breaker.

In the semifinals, the most dramatic play came when Gonzalez coldly and professionally executed Tilden, the performer. Meanwhile, double Grand Slam winner Laver battled single Grand Slam winner Budge. Laver won not with his slam but because Budge's awesome backhand drove naturally cross-court to Laver's strength—his southpaw forehand. In the final, Gonzalez triumphed when he made one stroke, his fearful serve, dominate a match as no other weapon could. Laver's skills remain unsurpassed, but a single lightning shot can defuse the most versatile arsenal. The Gonzalez serve did.

The women presented a difficult problem because Billie Jean King, Maria Bueno, Maureen Connolly, Margaret Court, Suzanne Lenglen and Helen Wills were so evenly matched. We confess weakness in choosing legend over icy statistics, but we chose Lenglen as champion.

The first round showed no surprises, though the Evert–Connolly encounter was entrancing. The score was short, but the rallies were long, as Maureen won, stolid and businesslike over Chris, stylish and graceful. Connolly won over Bueno in the quarters because the Brazilian's artistry could not overcome Connolly's smoothly churning groundstrokes. Court's physical conditioning wore down even such a staunch advocate of fitness as Helen Wills.

In the semifinals, King persevered over the meteoric Connolly. Court's loss to Lenglen and Lenglen's ultimate triumph over King are our irrepressible but improbable hope that the supreme artist would overcome the supreme athlete.

Billie Jean King.

NAME

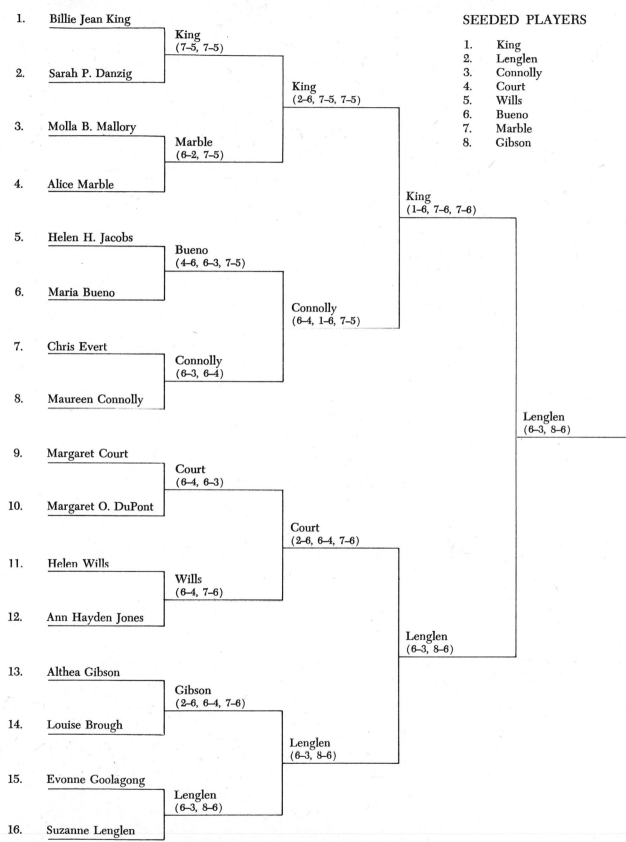

1. Billie Jean King

King
(7–5, 7–5)

2. Sarah P. Danzig

King
(2–6, 7–5, 7–5)

3. Molla B. Mallory

Marble
(6–2, 7–5)

4. Alice Marble

King
(1–6, 7–6, 7–6)

5. Helen H. Jacobs

Bueno
(4–6, 6–3, 7–5)

6. Maria Bueno

Connolly
(6–4, 1–6, 7–5)

7. Chris Evert

Connolly
(6–3, 6–4)

8. Maureen Connolly

Lenglen
(6–3, 8–6)

9. Margaret Court

Court
(6–4, 6–3)

10. Margaret O. DuPont

Court
(2–6, 6–4, 7–6)

11. Helen Wills

Wills
(6–4, 7–6)

12. Ann Hayden Jones

Lenglen
(6–3, 8–6)

13. Althea Gibson

Gibson
(2–6, 6–4, 7–6)

14. Louise Brough

Lenglen
(6–3, 8–6)

15. Evonne Goolagong

Lenglen
(6–3, 8–6)

16. Suzanne Lenglen

SEEDED PLAYERS

1. King
2. Lenglen
3. Connolly
4. Court
5. Wills
6. Bueno
7. Marble
8. Gibson

# Different Strokes

## A Portfolio of Modern Action

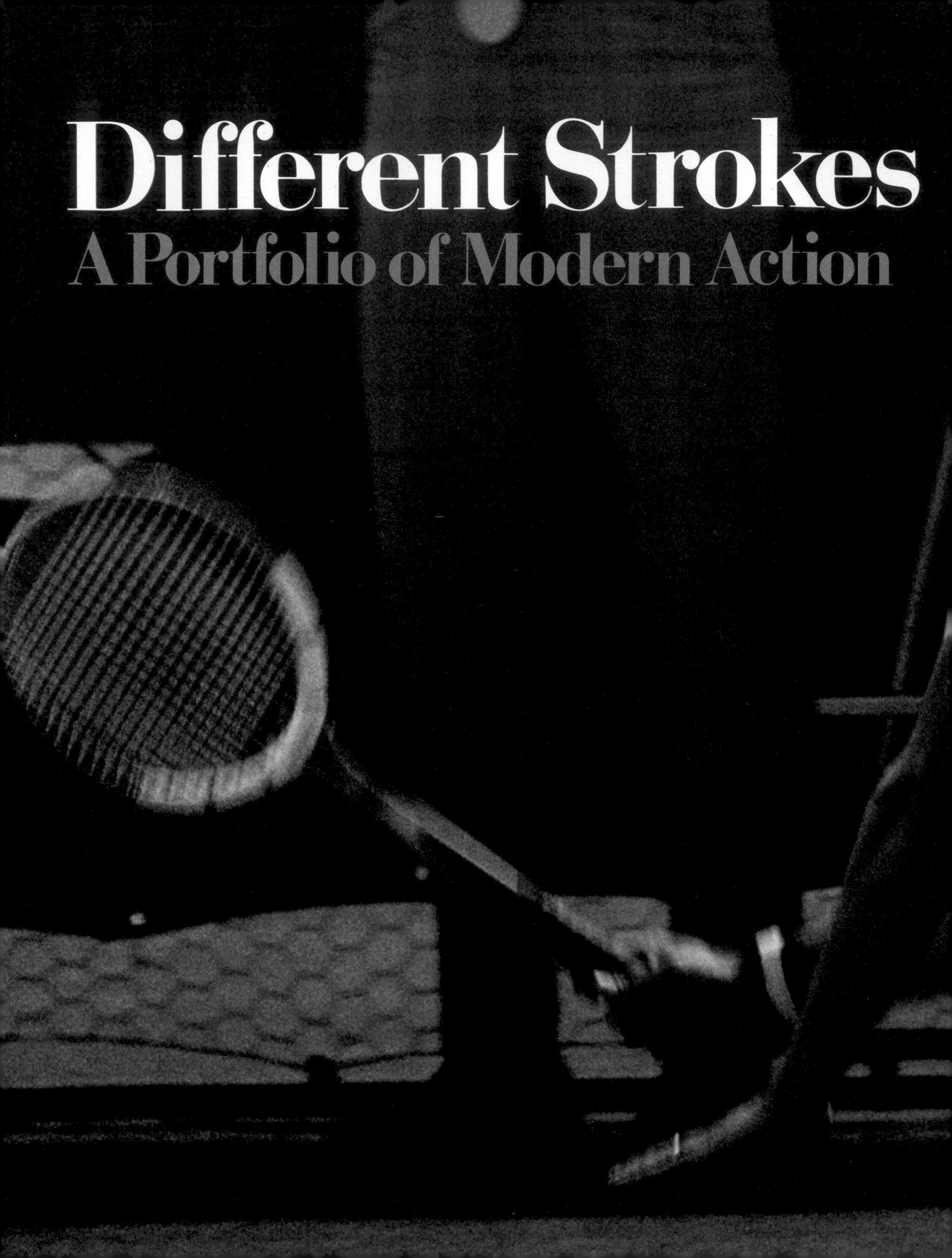

Ilie Nastase

Jeanne Evert

There is no sport with the expressiveness of tennis. Every professional has a different approach to each stroke. No two strokes are the same.
Nor are appearances the same. The athletes dress differently and react differently. These are the first of an infinity of fleeting impressions.

Tennis has its "bearded Dane," a modern mys-tic. He is tennis's guru, who experiments daily with grips, follow-throughs and new rhythms. Tennis has its very young, a 15-year-old who concentrates on a single method of socking a double-fisted backhand.

For the moment, they restrain their emotions, but a lucky let-cord or a linesman's errant decision could suddenly drive them to . . .

Torben Ulrich

fury . . . frustration . . .

concentration . . . controlled frenzy.

Ion Tiriac

199

Chris Evert

Andres Gimeno

Billie Jean King

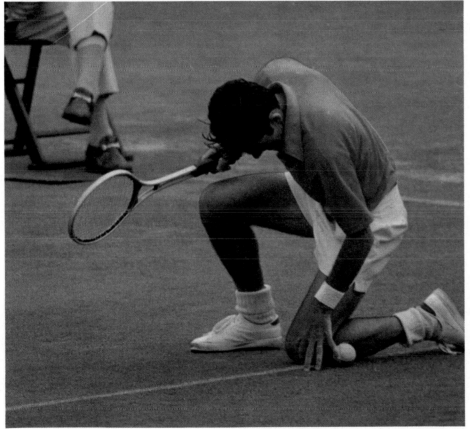

Ken Rosewall

The assortment of emotions and players are endless
—a youngster piqued, a Spaniard beseeching the
Almighty, a star distraught, Ken Rosewall's anger
silent as always.

For the pros, watching the ball is not a teacher's warning to a young student. It is an intense ritual. A professional is so highly trained that he can often hit strokes without looking. But he knows that such a concentration lapse is perilous. He quickly reverts to focusing on the ball, humbled like a beginner.

Julie Heldman

Tom Gorman

For all its spontaneous action, tennis maintains a sense of organization and meticulous precision.

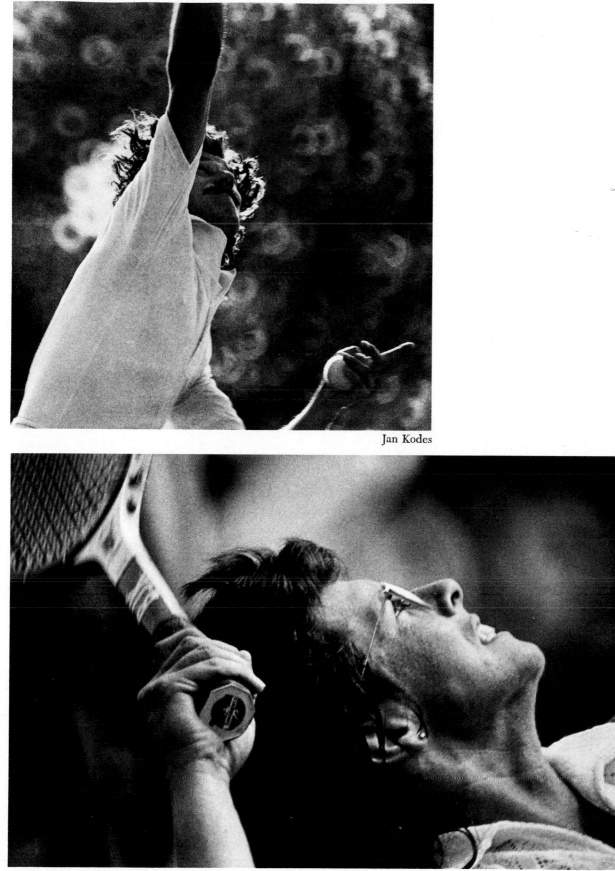

Jan Kodes

Billie Jean King

The serve once was supposed to merely put the ball in play.

Virginia Wade

Torben Ulrich

Fred Stolle

Today the serve sets up the wipe-out volley, and many times . . .

Rosemary Casals

Frank Froehling

sows destruction alone.

The pro's body endures punishing contortions. He stretches tall to serve, bends low to volley, some- times cramps for an overhead. Often a bizarre leap helps to control a forehand.

Valerie Ziegenfuss

Cynthia Doerner

Tennis constantly demands weird motion, wild
stretches and rigid concentration.

Rosemary Casals

Dick Dell

Margaret Court

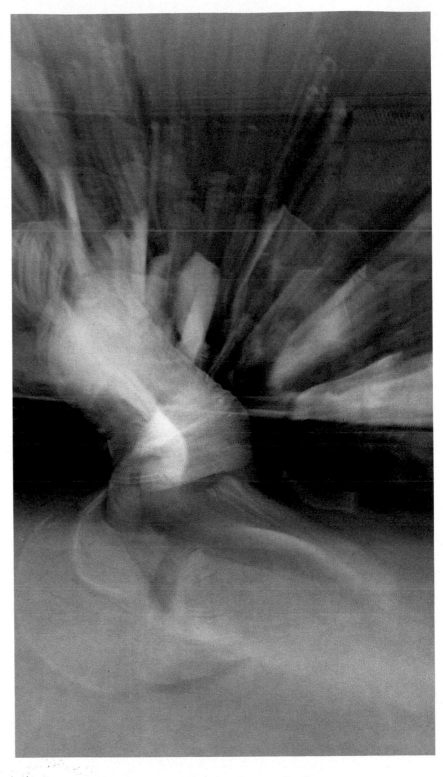

Despite moments of respite, tennis requires the fitness of a marathon runner, the agility of a gymnast, the concentration of a golfer and the strength of a shotputter. In a five-set match, a pro may run 20 miles, hit a ball 3,000 times and swelter under a wiltingly hot sun for four hours.

217

Valerie Ziegenfuss

Bob Lutz

Junko Sawamatzu

The strain is monstrous, the player's attention, riveting.

Billie Jean King's power, speed and balance is an awesome combination. Her aggressiveness is as pronounced off the court, where she has successfully fought for better playing conditions for women. She once played an exhibition against a man ranked tenth in America, was spotted 10 points and serve in a 21-point contest and lost, 21–17. Still, she suggests women's tennis is more interesting than men's because rallies are longer. Interspersed with Mrs. King's frenetic movements are moments of calm.

Derek Schroeder

Ilie Nastase

South African Derek Schroeder is a journeyman. Cliff Drysdale, once a South African, now a resident of Dallas, Texas, is the tour's intellectual, and formerly, its lover. Ilie Nastase is a gypsy with an angry, clowning, marauding, masquerading temper.

Cliff Drysdale

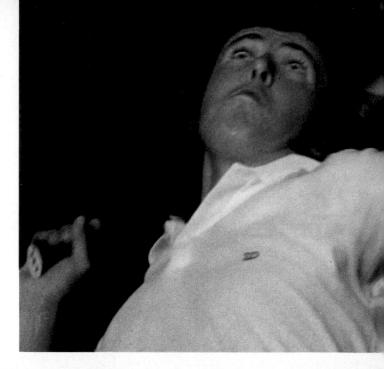

The variety is kaleidoscopic. Aussie Dent is the typical eager, bashing young pro. Olmedo is the old pro, a former Wimbledon and Australian champion, still willing to match his reputation against a feisty rookie. Tennessee's Tanner has an all-American boy image—handsome, powerful, blond hair.

Phil Dent

Roscoe Tanner

225

Alex Olmedo

An assortment of strokes: a backhand struck low, with almost no forward body motion, a high forehand, the player tilting impatiently toward the net . . .

Charles Pasarell

Olga Morozova

Lesley Hunt

Wendy Overton

a sweeping forehand, a stretching backhand, a scrambling volley.

Bob Lutz

Lesley Hunt

Aussie Hunt strokes a forehand close to her body. French stylist Durr hits the same shot straight-armed, away from her body.

Francoise Durr

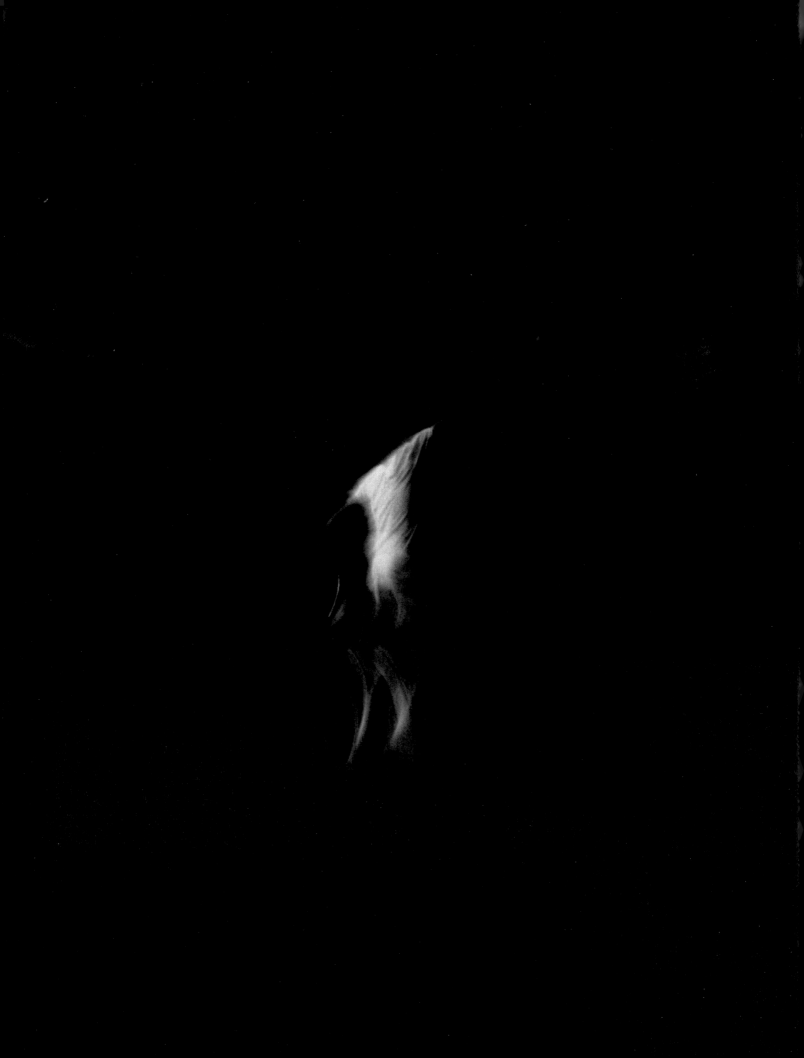

Marita Redondo

Amidst the force and frenzy there is serenity.

Competitive fury is not always anger. It is the true missionary's courage and zeal in facing the possibility that one's best may not be enough.

Bob McKinley

# A Gallery

# 9/ of Great Matches

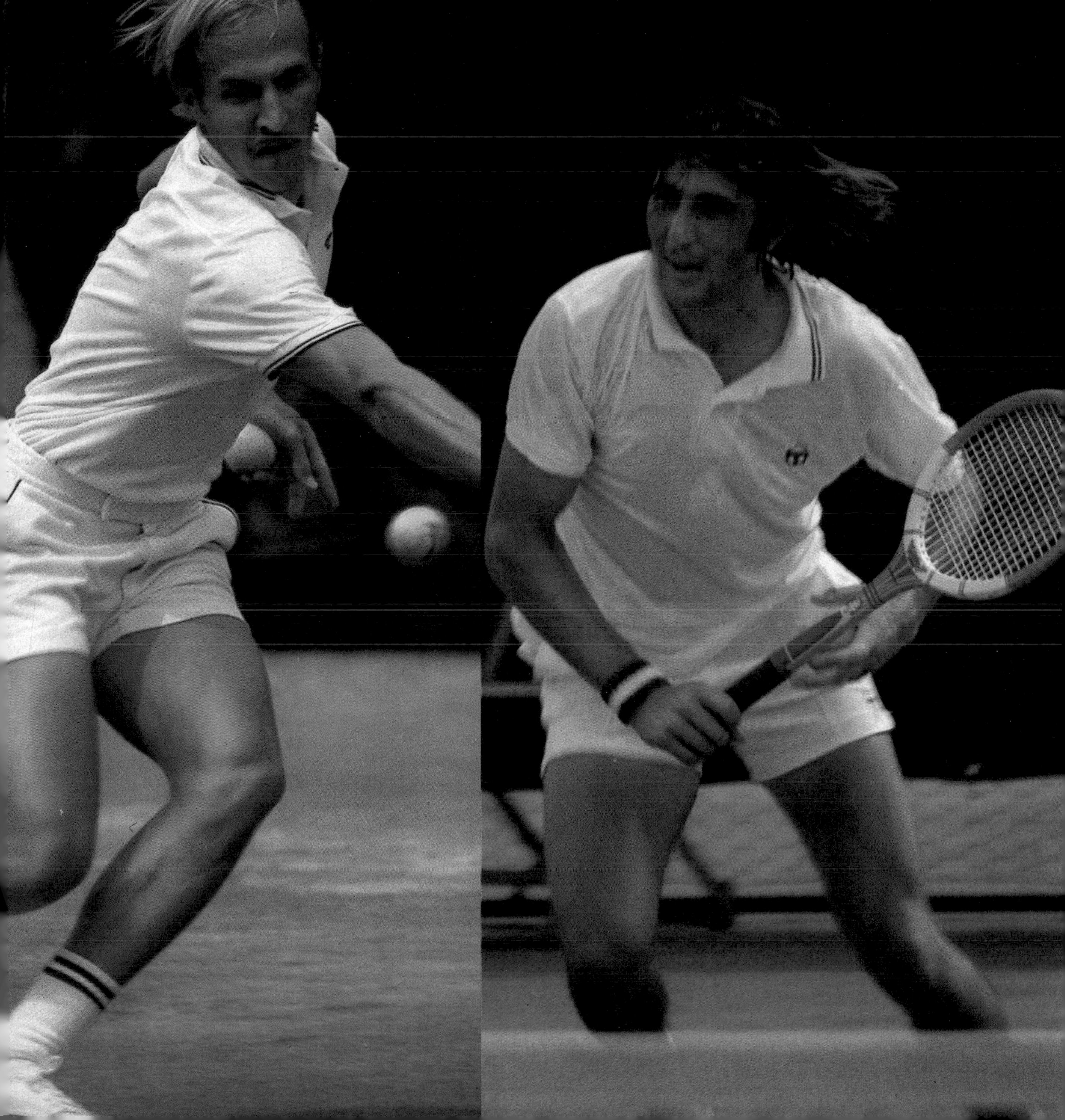

# Goolagong–Evert

From March 23, 1971, to September 7, 1971, Chris Evert played 46 tennis matches and did not lose. Many of her victims were junior contemporaries but not all; Billie Jean King, Françoise Durr, Virginia Wade, Winnie Shaw and Margaret Court all ranked among the top eight women players in the world. First, the Fort Lauderdale-tanned 16-year-old Evert was the heroine of the Wightman Cup, played on cement, a surface supposedly not to her liking. Then she won the Eastern Championships, on grass, a surface even more alien to her. The stage was set for Forest Hills, where the unseeded upstart staged one high-noon drama after another to storm into the semifinals. She came back from a one-set deficit three times, once miraculously saving six match points against Mary Ann Eisel.

Evert's meeting with Billie Jean almost rates inclusion in this list for the catatonic anticipation that gripped the Open before the match. Because of the excitement she generated at Forest Hills, Chris made the cover of *Newsweek* and the *New York Times Magazine,* the personification of innocence defeating hardened tour veterans. But against Billie Jean King, Chris found herself opposing a veteran who would rise to the challenge of a confident, young upstart. The champion tapped newly discovered energy with her throne imperiled and sent Chris home a loser, 6–2, 6–3.

Chris's match with King was part of the dramatic buildup to her enthralling encounter with Evonne Goolagong. In this instance, the outcome somehow was of secondary importance. Both women had their supporters, but the story of how each attained stardom before their inevitable confrontation was grand opera at its best.

For a year, while comparisons were artfully drawn, the girls knew only of each other's reputation. They had never met, even socially. Usually the top talent gathers at the same tournaments. But Jimmy Evert, Chris's father and a fine teaching pro himself, planned his daughter's schedule with the protectiveness of a fight manager. He had decided to keep his child well-rounded in a society that might spoil a young superathlete. Regular

schooling, no late nights and no extensive traveling were as important a part of Chris's training as two hours practicing cross-court backhands. As a result, Chris did not play the '71 European circuit and missed Wimbledon as well.

Evonne was guided by Vic Edwards, an Aussie coach, who became her foster father when she was 15. Vic's thoughts were similar to those of Jimmy Evert, his counterpart, except that he had allowed Evonne to turn professional. Chris was three years younger and an amateur. Edwards's training goal was to prepare his charge for a pro career, and the training reached fruition in 1971 when Evonne won Wimbledon. To win Forest Hills the same year would have been too much to expect, so Goolagong skipped the U.S. Open and returned to Australia.

A winter passed. Finally, in late April, the two girls entered the same event in Dallas and seemed destined to meet in the semifinals. But the seedings did not hold true, and both girls fell to older touring pros, who had grown tired of the attention concentrated on two youngsters. Appropriately then, the pair first met at Wimbledon, the ultimate stage for any tennis happening. Both picked their way cautiously but surely to the semifinals. Nothing more forestalled the epic confrontation.

A capacity crowd (15,000) focused its attention on the hallowed Centre Court. The contrast in styles of the two girls heightened the drama of the event. Chris Evert has a textbook backcourt game, heavily reliant on a two-fisted backhand. She rarely ventured to net but compensated for her lack of daring with intense concentration. Evonne, on the other hand, had a natural flair for the game.

In the beginning, both girls probed tentatively. Evonne's initial strategy to hit short, low balls to Evert's two-handed backhand sought to exploit the limited reach available for two-handed shots. But through power of concentration more than genius of stroke, Evert spurted from 2–all to a 5–2 and 30–love lead. Evonne was not yet in it, but her happy-go-lucky attitude even when behind had clearly won the heart of the crowd. Down 5–2, Goolagong gave a preview of her comeback prow-

*Evonne Goolagong* (opposite bottom) *and Chris Evert* (opposite top)
*met for the first time at Wimbledon in 1972, but the match itself could not equal the year-long
publicity that preceded it. Evonne won the semifinal, 4–6, 6–3, 6–4.*

ess as she bustled about, no longer awarding points through thoughtless errors but still not rising to the instinctive genius she was capable of. She won nine successive points to cut the margin to 4–5 and 15–love on her service. But a double fault interrupted her brilliant glow, and Chris pounced on the chance, winning the set on her third game point.

Because of its uneven bounce, grass is not a surface that invites long rallies, and control usually consists of simply keeping the ball in play. But Evert had the hand and eye of a surgeon, maneuvering the ball from corner to corner. Throughout the first set and the beginning of the second, Goolagong could only defend, letting Chris pattern the play.

Evonne responded not to danger, only to disaster. She was down 0–3 in the second set before inspiration began to wreck Evert's ball control. Suddenly, Goolagong was waiting for balls she had previously struggled to reach. With the anticipation of a seer, she floated quickly to net, dispatching volley winners outrageous in their boldness. She captured seven games running, winning the second set 6–3 and leading 1–0 in the final set before Chris momentarily checked her improvisational genius. Now the tempo of the match quickened as both girls slugged from the backcourt. Goolagong nosed in front, 4–3, but was quickly checked to 4–all.

One intuited that with the end near, fortune would favor the player not waiting for an error to win. At the finish Goolagong had the capacity to slap short or deep balls and follow her drives to net. Carefree to the end, she served at 4–all, losing only one point. The pressure not just of the day but perhaps of the year seemed to affect Chris more; she was plainly mentally exhausted. Evonne scooped a drop shot for 0–15, hit a forehand winner from backcourt and suddenly stood at match point. The last point summarized the struggle. With Goolagong at net, Evert sent a vicious cross-court drive, but Evonne flew to dispatch it and with it the match, 4–6, 6–3, 6–4. The crowd, seemingly stunned at the emphatic conclusion, rose slowly, clapping. Thus fell the curtain on a drama one year in the making.

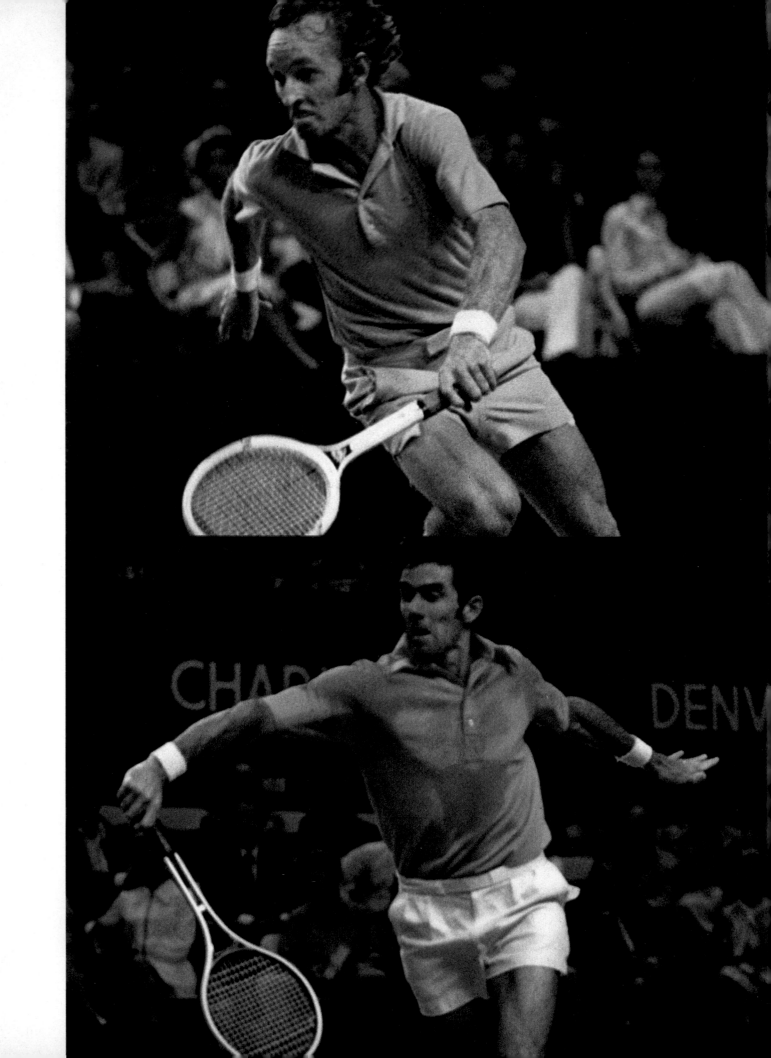

# Laver–Rosewall

The airless Moody Coliseum in Dallas seemed like a dusty street setting from a dime novel. The confrontation was stereotypically Western—two weary gunslingers tensed to shoot it out. Both Rod Laver, a left-handed, wristy shooter, and Ken Rosewall, a right-hand gunman, had terrorized Texas and the world, with their accurate blasts. But unlike gunslingers, they had faced each other countless times before on countless dusty streets, and probably they would again. The pair had met so many times that one's memory of the meetings and the scores had become blurred. The "Ken and Rod Show" had traveled to many a nameless city on Lamar Hunt's private tour for pros. The tennis was often superb but expectedly, boringly superb. Tennis needs new faces and new styles to keep it vibrant; Laver and Rosewall had become too common.

It took more than technically perfect tennis for the Rosewall–Laver final in May 1972 to achieve memorable status. This May match had all the elements of momentousness—the richest purse for a singles winner ($50,000), a magic if only theoretical title at stake ("the World Championship of Tennis"), the largest television audience in the history of tennis (21.3 million), two venerable stars as foes, both of whom had struggled to reach the final.

Both men were such excellent sportsmen that other than the sentimental observers, who favored Rosewall, only a handful much cared who won. Even the large cash prize didn't seem to goad the crowd into partisanship. Artificial lighting, the cramped and airless indoors, a synthetic playing surface gave the match a synthetic quality that only the level of play was able to transcend.

The match lasted three hours and forty-five minutes and five seemingly endless sets, the last two of which were resolved by tie breakers. Laver struck first and fast, off on a 5–1 binge before Rosewall could check his foe with a barrage of knifing backhand passes and telling volley thrusts. Rosewall's attempt to surmount the deficit came too late, and Laver closed out the first set, 6–4. But no man can successfully serve second serves for long against Rosewall's penetrating groundstrokes, and when

Laver's first serve deserted him, he paid the price. He tried to press on his second serve, which forced periodic double faults. Rosewall quickly routed his countryman in the next two sets, 6–0, 6–3. In the fourth set, so equally matched were the athletes off the ground and at net that in fairness the set should have ended a tie. It did, but the tie breaker was captured scrappily by Laver.

A quick service break by Rosewall in the last set gave inspiration to every "over-35er." But the man was tired. As Laver tied the set at 4–all, Rosewall dragged his feet between rallies, his shoulders stooped, his face drained. Rosewall always looks tired, and as he ages past his 38 years, it is certain that he will plaintively play the aged and infirm theme to unsuspecting, sympathetic foes. His shining black hair should serve as warning that he is an athlete who may never grow old, but he was truly exhausted as that fifth set wore on.

The rallies were a virtual syzygy. The server won his games not because of his natural advantage but because he struggled more mightily on service points than when he returned service. The pair were giving lessons in their contrasting styles; the carrot-topped left-hander all attack, Rosewall counterpunching in response. Leading 5–4 in the seemingly predestined tie breaker and needing only two service points to capture the crown, Laver assaulted the Rosewall backhand. Suddenly the script went awry. First one, then another backhand off serve flew past Rod for devastating winners. Now leading 6–5 in the tie breaker, Rosewall served, and Laver, dazed, plunked the serve into the net. The match was Rosewall's, 4–6, 6–0, 6–3, 6–7, 7–6.

The epic contest forecast part of the future of tennis. The indoor setting with blinding beacon lights, yellow balls, a synthetic, green carpet surface, one player in blue, the other in bright orange, all reminded one that the great god of television would be served. The eerie setting seemed to sound a warning not to lose the soul of an athlete's performance in a morass of wire and numbers. On this occasion it took a pair of fast-draw specialists to make it all human again.

*For the second time in as many years, Ken Rosewall (bottom) defeated Rod Laver (top) for the WCT $50,000 championship. Rosewall was totally exhausted after the match that many observers called the greatest ever played.*

# Smith–Nastase

The final round of a big tournament is a stage that somehow seldom produces the epic struggles of earlier rounds. Checking the accounts of the championship stage of major tournaments, one finds that the results are usually one-sided, dull or both. It is as if the last two survivors in a field of 128 are too exhausted from their trek to the finals to mightily contest the final leg. To many, being a finalist is glory enough.

In Stan Smith's encounter with Ilie Nastase in the 1972 Wimbledon finals, the standard of play throughout was extraordinarily high. The Smith–Nastase affair lasted five sets and two and a half hours, the proper quantitative ingredients for any memorable match. The preeminent Lance Tingay of the *London Daily Telegraph* concluded simply that "this final must rank among the finest ever played."

The contrast between the two men could not have been more striking. Smith supported a brutal serve and volley with straight ahead passing shots. There was no touch, no guile, no craft, to his game. Those are the prerogatives of Nastase, a lieutenant in the Romanian army, about whom the untrue rumor persists that he is the son of a Bucharest sheepherder.

In the opening set, both men probed each other's armor for chinks, but attacking, not probing, is Smith's forte. While Smith tentatively searched for the game plan that was so obvious it eluded him, Nastase threw enough topspin backhand passing strikes to win the first set. The jolt reminded Stan, usually superlative on grass, where his talents lay. He began to take extra time before each service and rushed net with mountaineer spirit, taking the second and third sets, 6–3, 6–3. There was no lobbing over his head nor eluding his octopus reach with passing shots. With ruthless power he blunted Nastase's topspin lobs and uncanny anticipation.

At 4–all in the fourth set, with Stan seemingly

in command, Nastase struck again. He moaned over two line-calls and switched racquets twice, but his artistry reappeared. A lob stopped Smith in his tracks, and a forehand pass left the gallery gaping. Nastase had the break and served out the set.

At 2–all in the final set, Smith saved three break points, the last with a delicate drop volley plagiarized from Nastase. But for the most part, the players had returned to their familiar styles. With the wingspan of a condor, Smith seemed to trap volleys in a clawlike racquet and unceremoniously dump the ball over the net. Undaunted, Nastase served bullets and saved two match points at 4–5 with rapierlike volleys. He continued to drop winners into distant corners.

At 5–all the issue seemed unresolvable, much to the audience's discomfort. When Nastase won a point, the gallery was a giant smile. When Smith won, muted appreciation acknowledged the disciplined and ordered accomplishment. Nastase was genius and art. Smith was the American dream of perseverence, forthrightness, character, morality and discipline. These values are no longer revered, or so it seemed at Wimbledon. Nastase, brooding, cunning, flamboyant, was worshiped.

To polite applause, Smith held serve to lead, 6–5, in the final set. As Nastase served, electricity filled the air. A 40–love lead was quickly squandered before Smith's thunderous returns. At deuce Nastase's black eyes darted furiously. He saved three match points. On the fourth, Smith lobbed weakly, and Nastase, incredulous at yet another reprieve, glanced at Smith. The lapse was critical, for tennis vengefully punishes lapses in concentration. Nastase netted the easy, high, backhand volley to end the match. For a moment a hush of disbelief fell over the crowd. Then they rose in unison and gave way to long, emotional, cathartic applause.

When serve and volley are cast against the craft and spins of the Continental touch, the results may be dramatic even on grass, once the domain of American and Australian sluggers but now, as Nastase proved at Wimbledon, no longer feared by the best Europeans.

*After two-and-a-half hours and five sets, Stan Smith* (above) *finally subdued Ilie Nastase* (opposite) *in the 1972 Wimbledon finals. Smith's power won out over Nastase's finesse.*

# Budge–von Cramm

*The Budge–von Cramm match in 1937 was played on three levels—Budge v. von Cramm, United States v. Germany and the free world v. the onslaught of Hitler.*

It was a match between the two best players in the game, Don Budge and Baron Gottfried von Cramm, the glorious German ace. More important, it was America against Germany. Not only was the world's number-one tennis position at stake but national pride as well. In July 1937, America was still politically neutral, but nationalistic emotion ran high in both countries. In this interzone final of the Davis Cup, the winner would certainly win the Challenge Round because defending champion Britain had lost its finest player, Fred Perry, to the professional ranks.

The United States and Germany were tied at two matches each when Budge and von Cramm walked through the majestic portals leading to Wimbledon's Centre Court. Above those portals still hangs an oak plaque with a Rudyard Kipling exhortation to "meet triumph and disaster and treat those two imposters just the same." Von Cramm was a known anti-Nazi and no doubt preferred Kipling to the Führer, who had telephoned the Wimbledon locker room to emphasize to him the significance of winning for the Fatherland. Budge remembered that "Gottfried came out pale and serious and played as if his life depended on every point." There would be no return call if von Cramm lost.

The proud German began the match like a runaway tractor, grinding up Budge's revered backhand drive. Von Cramm snatched the first set, 8–6, and the second, 7–5, by keeping Budge in backcourt with well-paced and well-directed groundstrokes. Both men were playing superior percentage tennis on grass—miraculous considering the irregular bounce on the surface and the extraordinary speed of Wimbledon's slick pitch. At the end, the umpire's chart showed that Budge had scored 115 placements, 19 aces and only 55 errors while von Cramm had 105 placements, 17 aces and 65 errors. Most tournament players never score more than 50 percent outright winners in any match. But superior statistics were no help to Budge, who needed to change his tactical approach to survive.

In the third set, he began to smack von Cramm's service on the rise and follow the return to net for the killing volley. Instantly successful, the tactic broke the German's service at 15 in the first game of the set. In the fourth game, Budge was overeager, and von Cramm shot four straight winners from service to tie the score at 2–all. But Budge broke back at love with a backhand rejoinder and rushed through his remaining service games to win the set, 6–4. After the 10-minute rest period, Budge rode momentum's easy wave through the fourth set, 6–2, to even the match at two sets each.

The match had started at 4 o'clock. It was now 7:30 P.M., and London's gray evening descended quickly with the slippery dew. The bounces were now virtual lightning. The extended rallies in the fading light, the ball almost invisible, created the weird effect of two semaphore operators conversing by means of their racquets.

The *Weltschmerz* welled in von Cramm, who sensed that only desperate adaptation could thwart Budge's onslaught. No adjustment was an easy one for the German aristocrat, who could not hurry his stroke and who had to be planted in position to fire his flat, backhand bolts. His facilely elegant game was troubled by an opponent on a streak of good fortune, for a certain lack of versatility prevented him from disrupting his foe's patterns. But von Cramm overcame his rigidity to force Budge's vulnerable forehand into two errors and the break, for 3–1. At 4–1 on the strength of a love service game, von Cramm grew impatient to close out the match, and, for the first time, his composure, usually so secure, was shaken, leaving him for an instant with only a nervous second serve. With the late-afternoon grass as slick as ice, only a miracle worker could have broken service at such a critical stage. Here, the Budge legend grew with every shot. His sickly forehand cured itself and ferreted openings as he boldly attacked the serve on four straight points to win the game at love. Then the American leveled at 4–all after surviving a game-point crisis with a forehand finisher that earlier in the match was unknown to him. At 6–all, the lack of variety that the baron had overcome in pressing his foe's once-frail forehand haunted him again. He attacked the forehand,

but instead of faltering under pressure, Budge's revitalized forehand forced two errors to break von Cramm's service at 15. Behind, 6–7, the baron braced to save three match points and then charged to break point. Deuce. Break point again. Deuce. Finally, Budge's fourth match point. In the final rally, Don Budge raced full tilt cross-court and hit a forehand thunderbolt down the line. At the end of the stroke, he sprawled ingloriously on the turf, leaving the whole court open for a winning reply. But there was none, so perfectly executed and placed was Budge's blast. It had scattered chalk dust from two lines and climaxed the struggle that has been called "the greatest tennis match of the ages."

The proud baron, without looking back, met Budge at net with unmistakable dignity. In a firm tone that gave no hint of anguish, he pronounced, "Absolutely the finest match I've ever played in my life. I'm happy I could play it against you whom I like so much."

# Lenglen–Wills

Of all the ballads sung at the story-telling summit meetings of sports, Dempsey–Tunney, Hogan–Snead, Ali–Frazier, Nicklaus–Palmer, none had the lyric qualities of the Suzanne Lenglen–Helen Wills confrontation at Cannes almost 50 years ago. The Evert–Goolagong match approaches it in anticipation, but the melody did not linger on. Modern sport is calculating in its theatrics, and as soon as the curtain comes down, one immediately turns to the rematch or the next spectacle, undoubtedly just around the corner. In the aftermath of Wills–Lenglen, there was ample time to savor and reflect, for the famous match at Cannes was the only time these two stars were to meet.

At 20, Helen Wills, "little Miss Poker Face," from California, was already touted as one of the great talents in tennis. Meanwhile, Mademoiselle Lenglen, even at the ripe age of 27, was acknowledged to be the finest woman player who ever lived. Though Suzanne was in and out of seclusion with almost comic regularity, her delicate temperament did not harm her performances on the French Riviera. She won every tournament on the Côte d'Azur, and throughout her entire career, she never lost a match in France.

American newspapers stirred the players as well as the public by insinuating that Lenglen's default at Wimbledon a year and a half earlier resulted from her fear of Wills. Though both sides of the Atlantic cried for a showdown, many thought it would never take place. This was tantamount to calling Lenglen a coward, an absurd assertion of journalists more familiar with covering opera stars than champion athletes. With such controversy the meeting became inevitable.

In early January 1926, Helen Wills left California and her studies for the French Riviera. The press speculated that Wills had taken the initiative and like a typically cocky American boldly taken the battle to Lenglen. It wasn't true, but it made good press. Wills wanted only topflight competition in the winter, and the only place to get it was in the south of France. She entered a tournament immediately, and despite an uneven performance while adjusting to the slow Continental clay, she won. Lenglen had not entered but did the following week at the Carlton Club in Cannes. The issue so hotly fanned by the press for more than two years was at last to be resolved.

The early rounds of the tournament were but a formality. The finals were the real attraction, and the atmosphere that surrounded them befitted a carnival. Special stands were erected that day to accommodate more than 4,000 fans. Ticket prices were raised to 300 francs ($12) for the day and were scalped for five times as much. Linesmen had been carefully selected, including Lord Charles Hope, a titled Englishman. If staged today by Madison Square Garden, the spectacle would have been a million-dollar promotion. The tension, already intense, was further heightened by a three-day rain delay.

In the beginning, from a 2–1 advantage by Wills, Lenglen strung 10 points together, went to 4–2, stuttered briefly to lose Wills's service but closed decisively at 6–3. Modern aficionados find it difficult to appreciate, but winning three games from Lenglen, who rarely lost a half-dozen points in any match, let alone a single game or set, was an event.

As in other such confrontations, the contrasting style of the protagonists added to the drama. Helen Wills projected a fierce competitive spirit, while Lenglen had the delicate temperament of a soprano. Lenglen's mother constantly traveled with Suzanne and quieted her prodigy's nerves with sugar cubes laced with brandy. It has been suggested that Madame Lenglen jangled more nerves than she soothed, and against Miss Wills, Suzanne eschewed sugar cubes and took her brandy from a glass between games. Her Gallic nose, oversized mouth and El Greco chin should have been an unsightly package; instead, her carriage and style made her attractive and elegant.

In the second set, Wills's service power did not allow Lenglen's finesse in the rallies to take effect. But even while falling behind, 1–3, Lenglen's craft was obvious. Not overpowering, she was uncannily accurate. Inexplicably, with a 4–1 lead in sight,

Wills slackened the pace and traded groundstrokes with Lenglen. Suzanne quickly leveled at 3–all. Wills again threw up her power gauntlet, the single answer to Lenglen's genius, and went to 5–4. But with such force, precision and accuracy are impossible to sustain. Lenglen leveled again at 5–all, went to 6–5 and match point at 40–15. An endless rally ensued before Wills finally pulverized a waist-high forehand. The cry "Out!" brought a victorious squeal from Lenglen, who went to net to receive the traditional handshake. The court was instantly mobbed, but somehow, through the chaos, Lord Charles Hope bulled his way to the umpire and explained that he hadn't made the call but that it had been shouted from the crowd. The umpire commanded that the court be cleared and play resumed. Lenglen was temporarily undone as she lost the game to be even at sixes. (It is reported that she never again spoke to Lord Hope.) Suzanne knew that if she lost the set, she was finished, so shallow were her reserves and so great her opponent's stamina. The uneven, sensitive but brilliant virtuoso steadied herself. She concluded the match in regal manner by lashing an outright winner that left Wills gaping in wonder. Suzanne's supple grace was suddenly serene and secure. The challenge was over, but the discussion of the match lingered on for that afternoon and others for endless seasons to come.

*Suzanne Lenglen and Helen Wills met for the first—and the last—time in 1926 in France, where Lenglen had never lost a match. Wills threatened, but the streak remained intact and would throughout Lenglen's career.*

# Nastase–Ashe

One of our prime standards for a great match is that it have significance beyond the points played and the champion crowned. Part of such significance comes when the match is played in a renowned forum. There have been many practice matches, involving Don Budge, Dick Savitt, Pancho Gonzalez, Rod Laver, Tony Roche and Ron Holmberg, which, if transferred to the Centre Court at Wimbledon, would rate a place among the best ever. One match in particular, between Whitney Reed and Rod Laver at Merion, Pennsylvania, 10 years ago, that Reed lost in five sets, was one of the most exciting ever played. Reed was the performer-athlete that tennis rarely experiences. Enormously popular in spite (or because) of his eccentricity, he was pitted at Merion against the world's number-one-ranked player. Reed lost, but narrowly, and produced an array of stick-'em-up backhands, falling-down forehands and behind-the-back volleys that enthralled the packed gallery. But as important as it was for Whitney, the match was not on a celebrated stage and must be relegated to the class of famous practice encounters, such as those between Budge and Savitt at the Town Tennis Club in New York.

Ilie Nastase produced his best in two major championship finals, while other champions or would-be champions performed disappointingly in such moments of potential high drama. Nastase is a magnificent athlete, who moves with such facility that spectators rarely notice how well he covers the court. He eschews the flashiness of a Chuck McKinley, one of the greatest court coverers, whose acrobatics never let one forget that he was an exceptional athlete. Nastase substitutes overly demonstrative behavior for his undemonstrative play. At a time when the subtle difference between colorful and rude behavior is not distinguished, Nastase has been the target of constant criticism for his on-court antics. Yet he is a free spirit, incapable of malevolent emotion. His playful nature is more the creature of his European mentality than of bad sportsmanship. He lost one heroic final in 1972. His victory at Forest Hills was a fitting comeback and just as dramatic as his loss at Wimbledon.

In 1972, for the first time in more than a year and a half, every top player was assembled at one setting—Forest Hills. Bitter administrative wars had separated the independent pros from their contract counterparts for almost two seasons. The public had become impatient, and now, at the U.S. Open, Laver, Rosewall, Newcombe, Ashe, Okker, Riessen, Lutz, Drysdale, Smith, Gimeno, Orantes and Kodes were all together.

Upsets decimated the mighty field. Laver lost to Richey, Rosewall to Cox, Okker to Tanner, Riessen to McMillan, Kodes to Mayer and Newcombe and Drysdale to Stolle. Only Arthur Ashe and Ilie Nastase survived. They met in neat confrontation for those to whom the old feud mattered; Ashe, the contract pro, versus Nastase, the independent. Ashe was a disciple of grass-court play, with a destructive serve and a wipe-out volley. Nastase was schooled on European clay courts and relied on speed, lightning reflexes, defense and counterattack.

Ashe started the match with the jangled nerves that are supposedly Nastase's infirmity. Arthur double-faulted twice in the opening game and dropped serve. Nastase, always the mimic, followed by double-faulting and also dropping service. The somber Ashe assaulted the Romanian's defenses, twice with backhand drives as hard as ever seen in Forest Hills's famed horseshoe. After squandering six break points, he won the first set, 6–3.

Rankled like a stallion, Nastase evened the score by counterpunching his foe's fastest drives to the corners and catapulting to net to conclude the volley. He had the second set, 6–3, but could not sustain his inspiration or his concentration and lost the third set in a decisive tie breaker. Nastase seemed undone. He had thrown a towel and hit a ball at a linesman. Ugly boos erupted from the stands, derisively exhorting the Romanian to "play tennis." Ashe, taking advantage of Nastase's absurd antics, led 4–2 and had another break point for 5–2 but missed by inches with a bold—perhaps too bold—return. With the match still apparently out of reach, Nastase loosened up his topspin and gave his mouth a respite. He went to work on Ashe's faltering serve, which was now mostly a second delivery. He had the break back in the eighth game and came alive with his own wrist-flicking attack. His simmering cauldron bubbled with mischief and genius. Two games later his uncanny anticipation distracted Ashe into muffing an easy volley and blowing the set, 6–4.

Ashe lashed out quickly and captured Nastase's serve in the first game of the final set, but the Romanian had not pressed accuracy on his first serve and sensed the tentativeness of Ashe's resurgence. He pressured the American's second serve to recap-

ture the service break. Memories of lost opportunities haunted Ashe. He only scored on his first serve when it didn't count. Nastase, a capricious blend of the blithe and the turbulent, dashed and danced constantly around the court as if nothing were at stake.

Nastase scored another break in the sixth game to lead, 4–2. Ashe had one last chance to get even when Nastase served, at 5–3. With Nastase at net, Ashe thundered a forehand at his foe's midsection only to see the ball return, blazing past him. It was quickly over, 3–6, 6–3, 6–7, 6–4, 6–3.

*The 1972 finals at Forest Hills pitted the psyching powers of Ilie Nastase against the icy cool of Arthur Ashe. For a while, Ashe's implacability prevailed, but in the end, it was Nastase's genius that proved decisive.*

# Hoad–Trabert

"Why did the crowd cheer my double fault?" Tony Trabert asked tearfully after losing the deciding match to Lew Hoad in the 1953 Davis Cup Challenge Round. "They're a pack of animals."

Davis Cup confrontations are more than personal struggles. In any individual championship, the pressure is enormous because of pride and the fear of humiliation in losing. When one loses, the loss is his country's as well as his own. For such reasons, Davis Cup encounters generate enormous misunderstanding, misunderstanding that underlies much of international tennis. The 1972 Challenge Round between the United States and Romania in Bucharest provided a dramatic example of how the once-lofty purpose of the Cup matches has eroded. Close line decisions consistently favored the home team as fairness was abandoned. Huge crowds noisily chanted the names of their heroes after every point, lustily cheered U.S. double faults and greeted American winners with icy silence.

It is a certainty that the Davis Cup schedule that now covers 8 months, 50 nations and 5 continents will be confined to 10 days in one country to accommodate the pocketbooks of pros, who lose money from the extended schedule. The obsession with the almighty dollar and superjingoism is a sad extension of the more benign fanatical aspects of the sport. Will moats and bulletproof barricades someday separate the tennis participants from the spectators?

In the December 1953, Challenge Round, Lew Hoad represented Australia with rare glory against American Tony Trabert. The strain on the husky, athletic American was monumental. America was not merely proud of Trabert—it had made its congenial star a virtual ambassador of international good will.

His team led the Aussies, 2–1, by virtue of his quick defeat of Ken Rosewall and his victory with Vic Seixas in doubles.

But Seixas lost the next day, evening the round. One more match would decide whether the cherished Cup would come to the United States or remain in Australia. The Kooyong Stadium was jammed with 17,000 loyal fans, the largest attendance ever at Melbourne. All Australia was glued to the radio.

Trabert had the build of a powerhouse halfback, and his decisive volley was a flashing rapier. He was U.S. champion, the premier player in the world, and the definitive favorite against Lew Hoad. His opponent, a 19-year-old Sydney-sider, was shorter than Trabert but blessed with the build of a blacksmith. The style of both was smoking power. No compromises, no subtlety, no guile.

The pair traded brutal serves and volleys for the first 22 games before there was a break. With a rush of driving returns, Hoad took the set, 13–11. It had lasted an hour and 20 minutes, longer than any of the preceding matches. While the Aussie gained in confidence, Trabert grew disheartened

and surrendered the second set, 6–3, watching a succession of untakeable serves thunder by. The gray overcast became a light rain, and the players donned spiked shoes. Trabert's experience slowly began to tell on the slippery turf. He varied the pace with sliced approach shots that stayed low and forced Hoad to hit up to the relentless Trabert volley. It was Hoad's first time in spikes, and he stumbled repeatedly on the slick turf. Trabert quickly won the next two sets, 6–2, 6–3.

Early in the fifth set, the tension unbearable, Trabert angled a nifty winner close to the net. Hoad, forgetting his spikes, tried to slide at the end of his lunge and crumpled in a heap at captain Harry Hopman's chair. Hopman casually flipped a towel at the youngster, who broke into a broad grin. The tension eased, but the Aussie struggled to hold serve, while the American batted aces in abundance.

The blockbuster hitting was so fierce that at one point Hoad socked the ball so hard that his racquet broke. Trabert volleyed the ball safely for the point, but the incident altered the match. Hoad fetched a new racquet with fresh strings and discovered that the new gut was more responsive than the old string, which had become sodden from the rain. His serve had new life, and he zipped an ace past the unknowing American to lead 6–5. In the next game Hoad took a love–30 lead and moved into position to attack Trabert's second serve. From the corner of his eye, Trabert saw his opponent's threatening movement and, apparently disconcerted, sent the second ball into the net. The crowd cheered the double fault. Triple match point. Trabert served again, and in a rare moment of caution, Hoad merely chipped a backhand that skimmed the net and landed at Trabert's feet. The American half-volleyed into the net, and Australia had retained the Davis Cup, 13–11, 6–3, 2–6, 3–6, 8–6.

Amidst the bitterness and controversy of the aftermath, both captains—Bill Talbert and Hopman—could agree that it was the most exciting Davis Cup match they had ever seen.

*The 1953 Davis Cup Challenge Round produced tennis of the highest quality as Tony Trabert met Australia's Lew Hoad. Hoad won the match, 13–11, 6–3, 2–6, 3–6, 8–6.*

# A Private Collection

There were other matches that had elements of magic or irony but that lacked historic significance. The rewards were no less for the spectators, but these were private experiences, reserved for those fortunate enough to watch in person, with no historical scribe to chisel the results in stone.

**Osuna–Santana:** The thrilling Rafael Osuna–Manolo Santana match at the 1963 Wimbledon would have rated inclusion in any list of great sports moments had it been a final. Instead, it was a preliminary match, but it left those who saw it with an unforgettable picture of the remarkable sleight-of-hand staged over five sets.

That Santana won, 2–6, 0–6, 6–1, 6–3, 6–4, is irrelevant. Perhaps there never before has been a match in which who won was of such little importance. Statistics support this point of view. Both men won the same number of games and, uniquely, the same number of points (132). It was a five-act drama with one player dominating each act until the last set when the virtuosity of both was equally on display.

In the opening sets, Osuna forged an enormous lead, though it was not as if the tennis itself were one-sided. The brilliance of the Mexican provoked tremendous shotmaking from Santana, who reached into his armament to first thrust and parry and then parry and thrust. For the first 50 minutes, Osuna was always on the winning end of these prolonged rallies. Drop shots, topsin lobs, angled volleys, stop volleys—all on parade. Down two sets to none, Santana could either pack it in or have a go. He chose the latter course.

He began to bank his forehand with noticeably more authority, and Osuna, the fastest man in tennis, was suddenly pressed to make returns that earlier had been candy and cake to reach. Santana's topspin backhand exploited the smallest opening. The third and fourth sets came easily to the Spaniard to square matters at 2–all.

There had been some errors on both sides—double faults, missed service returns—but that is the prerogative of the artist. Momentary lapses are but temporary valleys from which to climb to conspicuous heights. Momentum was still on Santana's side in the final stanza, and he soared to 4–1, then lapsed briefly to serve for the match at 5–3. Reenter Osuna. He chipped two backhand returns, the first causing a mistake outright, the second wedging an opening into which he slapped a volley winner. With a breathless stop volley, the Mexican had the break back. The grand artistry and sportmanship of both athletes seemed to defy fate to pick a winner. She chose Santana. His backhand pass in return of Osuna's searching first serve ended the match with a finality the gallery found difficult to accept. Applause rained on both men for a full five minutes before the audience reluctantly concluded there could be no encore.

**Tilden–Johnston:** Perhaps one fails to do justice to the legend of Bill Tilden by celebrating only one of his matches. He governed the game for more than 10 years with his volatile personality, as well as his play. He was an actor who chose stage center on all occasions. The one occasion we chose raised the curtain on his decade of dominance.

In September of 1920, World War I had left scars of destruction everywhere, even at the U.S. Championships final, where Tilden and regular foe Billy Johnston were waging their private war. A training flight plane had crashed not 200 yards away.

Johnston had won the championship the year before, but now Tilden's glory was to be proclaimed. "Big Bill" Tilden was a foot taller than "Little Bill" Johnston, and his service, which brought him 20 aces that afternoon, was a mile taller. Johnston double-faulted frequently and scored not a single ace. But at net, Johnston was Tilden's superior and would rap apparent passing shots back at Tilden's feet.

The match proceeded in perfect theatrical sequence; alternating winners and game scores through the first four sets, 6–1, 1–6, 7–5, 5–7. Tilden's innate flair for the dramatic repeatedly let victory slip from his grasp, but his service preeminence saved the match, 6–3, in the fifth set. With typical melodrama, Tilden catapulted to stardom.

**Drobny–Patty:** Seldom do marathon matches sustain excellence throughout, and equally seldom do they occur at an important championship. Not so when Jaroslav Drobny defeated Budge Patty, 8–6, 16–18, 3–6, 8–6, 12–10, at the 1953 Wimbledon. Not only did the match set a modern Wimbledon record of 93 games (later broken when Pancho Gonzalez defeated Charles Pasarell in 112 games in 1969) but the struggle was the final one between these rivals with a long history of bitter struggles. Both were legends at Wimbledon. Patty won it in 1950, and Drobny, the self-exiled Czech who first tried for the great English title in 1938, would finally win it in 1954. Both were enormously popular athletes. This particular meeting exposed the Centre Court gallery to a singular display of sporting play for more than four hours.

The contrast in styles was striking. Drobny projected the image of a heavy man with a heavy game and biting service, while Patty was more elegant in appearance and stately in tactical approach. When Patty won Wimbledon in 1950 and the customary dash of royalty appeared on Centre Court for the presentations, one had the distinct impression that the roles should have been reversed. Patty looked the part of the prince, and anyone around him, his servant. Except for Drobny. The no-nonsense Czech prevented the marathon match from being carried over to the next day when, at 10–all, he summoned unknown reserves to win, 12–10, in the fading light. Patty had characteristically gambled at six match points, but his crisp flat groundstrokes narrowly missed the mark. Applause rang down as if to toll the great rivalry and herald the memory of this match.

**Gonzalez–Pasarell:** On June 21, 1969, in the longest singles match ever played at Wimbledon, Richard ("Pancho") Gonzalez defeated Charles Pasarell 22–24, 1–6, 16–14, 6–3, 11–9. The match took five hours and twelve minutes and 112 games to play. The record will stand forever, for Wimbledon adopted the tie breaker in 1971 to curtail long matches.

Besides the record, the match destroyed the myth that tennis players, like track or swimming stars, are burned out at 30. Before the first Open in 1968, professional tennis was available only to the top amateur and a handful of supporting characters. If a young American athlete had not won the Nationals or made the Davis Cup team, there was enormous pressure to "settle down," quit tennis and get a serious job. This created the false impression that the players were retiring because they were over the hill.

After open tennis became a fact, the rush of professionalism created instant jobs. Tennis was now a respectable living. The over-30 players continued to compete and in many instances (Barry Mackay, Frank Froehling, Alex Olmedo, Mal Anderson, Neil Frazer and Frank Sedgman) came out of retirement. At Wimbledon Gonzalez demonstrated how mentally demanding the game really is and, perhaps, that it is impossible to master tennis in one's mid-20s. Forty-one-year-old Gonzalez outmaneuvered and outlasted twenty-five-year-old Pasarell. The old warhorse was the punctilious professor instructing in the arts of measured power, offensive lobs and percentage chip returns.

His chance to display professional wisdom almost never came. He trailed by two sets to love and complained the entire second set about the lack of light. It was 8:20 P.M. before play was finally postponed. Gonzalez came back the next day only to be immediately embroiled in another marathon set, which he finally won, 16–14. With fresh momentum, he took the fourth set as well, 6–3.

In the fifth set, the ageless Gonzalez blossomed again. He was down 4–5, love–40, triple match point, when his thunderous serve evened the score. At 5–6 he was down 0–40 again and replied curtly with an ace. Gonzalez survived one more crisis at 7–8 when Pasarell nervously lobbed over the baseline. After he salvaged each match point, one had the feeling that the great Gonzalez was somehow tricking Pasarell. His final sleight-of-hand was to

make Pasarell disappear. By bunching 11 points in a row from 9-all and winning his serve at love, Gonzalez captured the final set, 11–9.

**Vines–Crawford:** Ellsworth Vines was a meteor across the American tennis horizon. He flashed his brilliance in nifty triumphs at the U.S. Nationals in 1931 when he was only 19 years old. He added Wimbledon and another U.S. title in 1932. In 1933, Vines's bristling attack fired Wimbledon's Centre Court with a thunderous service and a lightning volley. He destroyed all opposition until the final round, when he met Jack Crawford.

For the first set, Crawford was only a passive witness to Vines's explosive thrusts that continually made the chalk fly. But Crawford dug in for the second set and captured it, 11–9, after successfully exploiting the technique of ramming the service return on the rise and boldly rushing the net. Disheartened, Vines surrendered the third set as well but stirred himself for the fourth (while his foe's resistance weakened) to even the match at two sets apiece.

Continuing to probe the attacking armor of his adversary, Crawford discovered success in taking the ball early and hitting to Vines's backhand. At 4–5 Crawford penetrated Vines's serving power by blocking the ball into play and waiting for the true opening instead of shooting for the outright winner. In a four-point burst, Crawford broke Vines at love and won, 4–6, 11–9, 6–2, 2–6, 6–4.

By late 1933, at the still tender age of 21, Vines

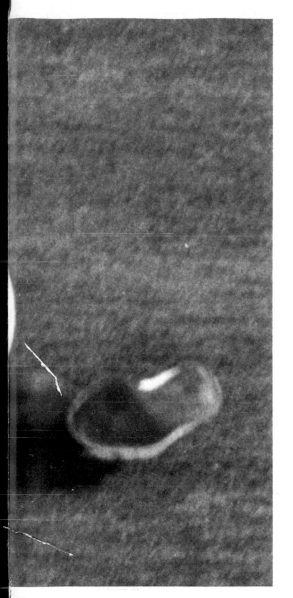

had begun his descent, and he turned to the less-demanding pro ranks of the time. Some say Ellsworth Vines at his prime was the greatest tennis player who ever lived. The 1933 Wimbledon final between Vines and Crawford, the resourceful Australian, is a rebuttal to that point. Vines lost to an inspired Crawford, whose game was traditional and stately rather than innovative. The Vines–Crawford encounter was not disastrous for the precocious Californian. It merely tinged with mortality (and reality) another legend and chastened its proponents.

Opposite and above: *Pancho Gonzalez*